Weight Training for Martial Artists

by
Jennifer Lawler

Weight Training for Martial Artists

by
Jennifer Lawler

Turtle Press   Hartford

To contact the author or order additional copies of this book:
Turtle Press
401 Silas Deane Hwy.
PO Box 290206
Wethersfield, CT 06129-0206
1-800-778-8785

Cover photography by Jon Walton
Cover model: Michael Tennier
Cover design by Tamara Dever

ISBN   1-880336-23-5
First Edition
Library of Congress Number 98-38644

Cataloging in Publication data

Lawler, Jennifer
        Weight training for martial arts / by Jennifer Lawler. -- 1st ed.
            p.   cm.
        Includes index.
        ISBN 1-880336-23-5
        1. Martial arts--Training. 2. Weight training.   I. Title
GV1102.7.T7L39   1998   98-38644
    613.7' 13--dc21

Contents

Introduction

If you've picked up this book, it's because you're a martial artist or an aspiring martial artist and you want to increase your strength. Most martial artists know their techniques will be more powerful and more explosive if they add weight training to their workout regimen. But many martial artists hesitate to get involved in weight training because they are afraid the added muscle mass will slow them down and reduce their flexibility. They may also be afraid that taking time to lift weights will take away from the amount of time they have to practice the martial arts.

But that doesn't have to be the case. You can use weight training to increase your power and explosiveness without compromising the speed and flexibility you've worked so hard to achieve. And the time you devote to weight training will be worth it. In fact, weight training can give you an edge in the martial arts that you can't get any other way. It's just a matter of how you train.

Another concern martial artists have is becoming too bulked up. They may not find the huge body builder physique very appealing. This is especially true for female martial artists. But you can become stronger with harder, better defined muscles without adding a lot of bulky muscle mass. Unless you plan to devote fanatical attention to weight training, you don't need to worry about bulking up. How you lift will determine how big your muscles get.

By following one of the plans suggested in this book, you can become a stronger, more explosive martial artist without sacrificing speed and flexibility. You'll be more toned, have more muscle endurance and be able to perform your martial arts techniques better than ever.

This book offers weight training flexibility for martial artists by offering a variety of approaches designed to help you create the best weight training program for your needs. The martial artist's weight training workout has a number of features:

• flexible plans depending on how much time is available for weight training;

• warms ups and stretches designed to prevent common injuries;

• exercises tied to corresponding martial arts skills;

• proper technique demonstrated, to promote strength building;

• flexibility training incorporated into the lifting programs;

• isometric and isotonic exercises provided for individuals without access to weights;

• traditional martial arts strength training exercises described for interested martial artists;

• lifting programs designed to meet the needs of specific martial arts;

• workout plans that focus on one aspect of conditioning;

• completely customizable training programs to fit the preferences of any martial artist.

Plus, the book includes a special chapter on injury prevention/ treatment and a special appendix with a training log.

Weight Training Basics

The martial artist's weight training program is a fully customizable plan for improving strength while maintaining speed and flexibility. It can be adapted to meet your needs, skills, goals—it even takes into consideration the martial arts style you practice.

Weight Training Basics

To get the most from this program, you need to understand the basics of weight training and the different theories that explain how weight training works and how the best results can be achieved. Chapters One and Two provide that information. If you are already familiar with weight training, you may wish to skip to Chapter Three to learn more about how to incorporate lifting into your martial arts workout. But even experienced weight lifters can benefit from a review of weight training fundamentals.

Strength training is usually done through lifting weights, but some strength training can be achieved without using weights at all. The main key to building strength and muscle is resistance. Whenever you deliberately work your muscles against resistance, they can grow stronger. As long as you provide resistance for your muscles, you can build strength. Resistance can be provided in a variety of ways, but lifting weights is one of the most efficient methods for doing so. Other ways to build strength are described in Chapter Three.

Because lifting weights is one of the most effective ways to increase strength, the training programs shown in this book require access to weights. You don't need to belong to an expensive gym or be intimidated by the weight lifters you see at your workout facility. You can do weight lifting at home with a minimal investment. However, some people do choose to work out at a gym because the facilities allow them a wide range of weight lifting equipment, plus other exercise equipment they might use, such as stair machines and treadmills for aerobic workouts.

Weight Training Approaches

To increase your strength, you can follow one of several approaches, or you can combine several approaches. You can use *free weights*, like *barbells* and *dumbbells,* or you can use *weight machines*. Free weights are metal bars with weighted plates attached to the end. *Dumbbells* are small, meant to be lifted with one hand; *barbells* are longer, meant to be lifted with both hands. The weighted plates are attached to each end of the bar with a clip or collar so that they don't slide off when you pick up the bar.

You can also use weight machines. These are often referred to as Nautilus® or Universal® machines, although there are many different brands. Weight machines have a stack of weight plates permanently set in place. You simply select the weight you want to use by setting a pin in the stack of plates at the appropriate weight mark. You then lift the weights by lifting or pushing on a bar or a set of handles.

Strength Training Methods

Free Weights: Barbells, Dumbbells

Weight Machines: Nautilus®, Universal®

Traditional: Dynamic tension, Makiwara

Isometric: Crunches, Pull-ups

Free Weights Vs. Weight Machines

Lifters disagree on which is the better choice—weight machines or free weights. You won't see a lot of body builders using weight machines (except perhaps for some exercises), but as a martial artist, you don't necessarily want to be a body builder. Still, free weights have certain advantages. Because you have to do all of the balancing of a free weight, you work a lot of muscles during any one lift, especially the smaller, stabilizer muscles that are difficult to work out otherwise. Free weights require equal strength on both sides of your body. When you lift a barbell, your left arm must work as hard as your right arm to keep the bar straight. A stronger arm can't compensate for a weaker one, as can happen with weight machines. Free weights are also flexible. You can do hundreds of exercises with a set of free weights, whereas weight machines are designed to do only one or two exercises each. Also, you have more than one way of doing an exercise with free weights, which may make the workout more comfortable and more rewarding. Finally, you can pile a lot of weights onto a barbell or a dumbbell, whereas you are limited in the amount you can lift with a weight machine.

There are some advantages to weight machines as well. They're safer to use. You're not going to drop a weight machine on your foot or on your chest. For this reason, you don't need a spotter as you often do with free weights. Weight machines are easy to get the hang of, too. They don't require a lot of experience to use, so you're more likely to use them correctly. Also, you can isolate and work on just one muscle at a time on a weight machine. This way, you actually work your biceps instead of your shoulder or vice versa. Finally, since the weights on a weight machine are easy to change, your workout can go faster and more smoothly.

You can also use traditional martial arts methods of strength training. These require very little investment, but they can sometimes be dangerous for novices. Chapter Three describes some of these methods in more detail.

Finally, you can build strength without weights by using your own body to provide resistance. For example, you can do crunches and push ups to improve your strength, as well as other exercises that can help you get explosive power. Isometric exercises can be used when you don't have access to weights, like when you're traveling.

For the martial artist, the best approach to strength training is to combine all of these approaches. Using weight machines, free weights, isometric exercises and traditional methods of strength training gives you a workout you can't achieve any other way. By combining these different approaches, you will reap all of the benefits of each method without suffering the drawbacks. Of course, you may wonder how you can do all this and still keep your job, but there are plenty of ways to pack even a short workout full of muscle building strategies and exercises.

Free Weights	Weight Machines
Advantages:	**Advantages:**
Work many muscles	Safe to use
Work smaller muscle groups	Often don't need a spotter
Flexible, easy to store	Easy to learn
Can handle a lot of weight	Easy to isolate one area
Build strength equally	No need to change weights
Disadvantages:	**Disadvantages:**
Have to change weights often	Limited number of exercises
Require some practice	Easy to "cheat"
Require a spotter	Limited weight stack
Can be dropped	Take up a lot of space
	Expensive for home use

Choosing a Fitness Center

If you do decide to sign up for membership at a gym, make sure you find a place that's convenient (otherwise you might have trouble getting your workout in) with a knowledgeable staff. You should never be afraid to ask questions about the exercises you are doing, the machines you are using or any other fitness related question.

Before you sign up, be certain you know exactly how much a membership costs, what it entitles you to, and whether you can get a refund or a credit should you become sick, injured or pregnant—that is, unable to work out at the gym. You also want to make sure the staff is qualified to answer your questions. (You want to be certain they can advise you appropriately about lifting correctly and other related concerns.)

The fitness center should be clean and the equipment should be in good shape. Check the hours they're open and when they're the busiest. Visit at a time when you would be most likely to work out. Is the place very busy? Will you have access to the equipment right away or will you have to wait for a long time to use each machine or to get a bench?

Spending the time to investigate different gyms can help you choose the right fitness facility for your weight training workouts.

Keep in mind that a number of martial arts schools have weights (either free weights or weight machines) available for their martial arts students to use. If this option is open to you, it can be a real time and money saver. You can do your weight training workout before or after your martial arts workout to save time, and the use of the weights is usually free or requires just a small monthly fee.

Choosing Weight Training Equipment

You may decide to do your weight training at home. Or, you may wish to have some weight lifting gear at home to supplement the workouts you get at the gym. If that's the case, then you'll want to choose your equipment wisely to get the most for your money. You can find weight training equipment at most major sporting goods stores. Dumbbells and barbells can be purchased with fixed weights or with adjustable weights. With the fixed weights, of course, you don't have to change out the weight plates every time you do a different exercise. However, since you'll need fixed weights in a variety of sizes, this may be a more expensive proposition than purchasing an empty bar and clipping weight plates to it. Expect to spend between $.50 and $2.00 a pound. Plastic coated dumbbells can be easier on your hands than plain metal ones, but the plastic can rip over time.   Quality doesn't vary that much among free weight sets, but always test before you buy to make certain that the collars stay snug and the weight plates don't rattle.

The same holds true for the barbell. You can either get fixed weight barbells (which aren't very practical) or you can get an adjustable weight barbell that allows you to clip different weight plates to it. Barbell weight plates cost about the same as dumbbell weight plates.

If you decide to purchase free weights, it's always best to start with dumbbells. Once you have a good set of these and have some extra money to burn, then you can invest in a barbell or two. It's possible to purchase adjustable weight sets that come with one barbell bar and two dumbbell bars, plus an assortment of weight plates that fit both the dumbbell bars and the barbell bar. This is probably the least expensive option.

The drawback to adjustable free weights is that the weight plates on adjustable free weights tend to rattle around a lot, and sometimes the collars aren't very good at keeping the plates on. Also, it can be a bit time consuming to add on and take off the weights for every exercise. The fixed weight free weights are more expensive and take up more room but they're more convenient to use.

If you do purchase free weights, you might want to purchase a rack for storage, so that you aren't constantly tripping over weight plates and bars. Racks can be almost as expensive as a set of free weights, so if your weight room is in the basement, you don't need to bother. If, however, the weight room also doubles as the living room, it might be a good idea to invest in a rack.

You should invest in a weight bench. These allow you to do many exercises that are otherwise impossible to do with free weights. A flat padded bench can cost around $100. One that inclines will start at about $175. If you have the extra money, go for the incline bench, because it is much more versatile than the flat bench.

Free weights, racks and benches can often be found at garage sales and used sporting goods shops for considerably less than you would pay retail. This can sometimes be a good choice for lifters on a limited budget, but be certain that the goods are in decent shape. Check to make sure that the collars on free weights lock shut so that you don't have weight plates bouncing off the dining room floor. Also, if you purchase a used bench, make certain it's still stable and is easy to adjust (if it's the incline variety).

You can purchase a weight machine for use at home, although this is a much more expensive option than purchasing free weights. Also, you have to make the investment all at one time. Weight machines for home use are called multi-gyms, because they have multiple exercises for you to do. Although you want a machine that's flexible, there are a few more important things to consider when buying a home weight machine. First, you want to purchase a machine that has a weight stack (two is ideal) with at least one or two hundred pounds of weight. If you are able to purchase a machine with two weight stacks, more than one person can use the machine at a time, which can make the work out more fun. Don't go for machines that use flexible tubes or rubber bands for resistance. They don't offer the same amount of resistance as regular weight plates do (no matter what their advertisers say) and tubes and bands don't wear as well as weight plates do.

Make sure the cables are durable, preferably coated nylon, not chains. Chains can crimp and get stuck. Make sure the seat and handles are easy to adjust for each exercise. Finally, try out the weight stack to be certain that it moves smoothly regardless of the amount of weight you're lifting.

Although a weight machine is more convenient than free weights, it takes up a lot of room (regardless of what the ads say about folding up for convenient storage). So if you're in a small space, a weight machine is probably not a good choice for you.

Wrist Weights, Ankle Weights and Weight Vests

Martial artists interested in building their strength often consider purchasing ankle weights, wrist weights and weight vests. Ankle weights and wrist weights are flexible weights that strap to the ankle or the wrist in order to provide resistance. Weight vests are vests made of canvas or nylon with pockets that accept special weights. All of these types of weights are supposed to be used while doing other exercises, such as jogging.

Although there isn't anything inherently wrong with these types of weights, they probably won't do you a lot of good. Most wrist and ankle weights weigh five pounds or less, which isn't enough to challenge your muscles to become stronger. This is true even if you simply want to tone and firm your body. In addition, you need to use different amounts of weight for every exercise you do, since each muscle or muscle group requires a different weight to challenge it. Finally, these weights can be hard on your joints, especially if you simply wear them around the house in hopes that they'll magically increase your strength.

Weight vests tend to weigh a little more than ankle and wrists weights, but since you're not exactly working your muscles against resistance when you're wearing one, they aren't as effective as simply lifting weights. Think of it as the difference between carrying a twenty-pound kid around for a few minutes and lifting the same twenty-pound kid ten times in a row. Although they need to be used with caution, these weight devices aren't necessarily bad. It's just that there are better ways to increase your strength.

Getting Started

Once you've decided to add strength training to your workout routine, you'll come across a lot of different theories about how to get the optimum workout. These theories are discussed in Chapter Two. To understand them, you need to know some basic information such as the definitions of words like *rep* and *set*. The word *rep* is short for *repetition*, and it simply means a doing a single exercise one time. Therefore, one rep means doing an exercise (such as a Leg Extension) one time. Two reps means twice and so on. This is important because the number of reps you do is related to your weight lifting goals.

The word *set* refers to the group of repetitions you do for any exercise. For example, if you do ten Leg Extensions before resting, your *set* consists of ten *reps*. If you rest for a minute and then do ten more Leg Extensions before moving on to the Chest Press, you've done two sets of ten reps each. Sets are important because the number of sets you do is also related to your weight lifting goals.

A *routine* or *regimen*, sometimes called a *program*, simply refers to everything you do during a weight training session. This can change from day to day as you try to challenge your muscles to grow stronger. Starting in Chapter Four, a wide variety of weight lifting routines are described to help you to find one that meets your needs.

Setting Weight Training Goals

Before you start any weight training or fitness program, you should check with your doctor first. You may have some specific physical conditions that would make it unwise for you to lift weights. Even if you are in good physical health, if you have injured your back or knees in the past, seek your physician's approval before starting a weight training program. If at any time during weight training you feel pain or suspect that you have injured yourself, you should stop what you are doing and consult with your doctor before starting again. See Chapter Seven for tips on injury prevention.

To start lifting, you need to have an idea of your goals. This helps you plan your overall weight training strategy. For instance, if you want to add a lot of muscle bulk, your plan should be different from someone who wants a more toned body. To achieve your goals, it's important to understand how weight training shapes your muscles.

Doing the Correct Number of Reps

Toning: 8-15 reps

Martial Arts Training: 10-12 reps

Bulking Up: 5-9 reps

How Weight Training Works

Whenever you lift weights, you are actually tearing down the muscle fibers in the targeted area. As those muscle fibers heal, they become thicker and stronger. Therefore, the more weight you lift, the more you stimulate your muscles to grow thicker and stronger. If you lift less weight, you will still stimulate muscle teardown and regrowth, but it won't be as obvious. That's why many people choose this last option: lifting less weight equals toned but not bulky muscles.

Your goal on every set of exercises is to work your muscle or muscle group so that the last repetition is difficult to do. For people looking to build a lot of bulk, the general rule of thumb is to work the muscle to failure, which means it simply cannot move any more weight without a rest. This doesn't mean, however, that you should do twenty-five repetitions of an exercise until you get tired. This is unlikely to stimulate muscle growth. It is generally accepted that toning and defining muscles requires between eight and fifteen repetitions of each exercise. Ten to twelve is usually thought of as ideal. This means that you should lift enough weight so that it is very challenging to complete that last repetition. As you grow stronger, you will add additional weight so that the last repetition always remains a challenge to complete. A program that follows these guidelines is excellent for muscle endurance, which means your muscles can perform difficult tasks for longer periods of time. For a martial artist, muscle endurance is as important as stamina or cardiovascular endurance.

To produce a stronger, more muscular look, you want to limit your repetitions to between five and nine, with about six being ideal. Again, your last repetition should be very difficult to do. This means that you're lifting a much heavier weight than if you were doing ten or twelve repetitions. This stimulates your muscles to grow bigger and thicker. However, lifting heavier weights fewer times doesn't increase your muscle endurance, so unless a really powerful body is your goal, most martial artists should aim for the ten-to-twelve rep range.

If you really want to add some bulk, you can train like body builders and power lifters do, and that is to lift as much weight as possible for only one or two repetitions. Although this is not recommended for martial artists, as too much bulk can indeed slow you down and impair your flexibility, it can be a good strength test to try every now and then.

Lifting Weights Correctly

Each repetition of an exercise should be done smoothly and evenly without bouncing or jerking movements. It should take about the same amount of time to lift the weight as to lower it. There should be no pause between lifting and lowering the weight. Doing so can be very stressful on your joints. Most experts believe that each exercise should take about four or five seconds to perform. At first, you might count as you perform each lift until you find a good pace.

You also need to breathe correctly when you perform a repetition. Although body builders use special breathing exercises, most lifters simply need to remember to breathe while lifting. It isn't uncommon to see untrained lifters holding their breath as they perform their exercises. This is very dangerous, since it can actually cause a spike in blood pressure, which is hard on the heart. Also, physicians say that they sometimes see collapsed lungs in weight lifters who don't breathe correctly when they work out. A good rule of thumb is to exhale during the part of the exercise the requires the most exertion. This prevents you from holding your breath as you lift. During the lowering or less difficult part of the exercise, concentrate on inhaling. By concentrating on your breathing, you can avoid some risks of lifting and you can find a good, even rhythm for your exercises.

Tips for Lifting Weights Correctly

1. Each rep should be done smoothly.

2. Do not bounce or jerk the weight.

3. Take about the same amount of time to lift and lower the weight.

4. Do not pause between lifting and lowering the weight.

5. Take about 4 to 5 seconds to perform each rep.

6. Breath with each exercise: exhale during exertion, inhale during the less demanding portion of the exercise.

7. Start with lighter weights and work up to your capacity.

8. Keep a training log to track your progress.

9. Start with one set of reps for each exercise. As you progress add a second set.

10. Use a spotter when necessary.

11. Do not work the same set of muscles two days in a row.

Where to Start

Of course, finding the right amount of weight to lift requires a bit of experimentation. When you begin your weight training program, start with lower weights and build up to your capacity. By keeping a training log you can track your progress. This way, you don't stand over the Leg Extension machine scratching your head and wondering how much weight you lifted last time. As you start a weight lifting program, you'll want to stick with one set of repetitions for each exercise. This may be all that you ever have to do. However, if you want to add more muscle or if you feel you need to challenge yourself in your workout, you may want to add another set of each exercise. You can do this by going through your whole routine twice, or you can do it by performing one set of reps, then resting for a minute and then performing a second set of reps. Don't be surprised if you can't lift as much weight or complete as many reps in the second set. You'll have to build up to it (this is another reason why keeping a log can help you keep track of what you're doing). Serious weight lifters will do five or ten or more sets to stimulate muscle growth.

Spotting and Free Weights

If you're using free weights, you will sometimes need a *spotter* (and you'll occasionally be asked to spot). *Spotting* simply means helping someone with their lifts. For instance, a person may be performing a Chest Press by using a barbell while lying on their back on a weight bench. Since the lifter wants the last repetition to be challenging, he or she may get into trouble and be unable to hold the barbell up. That's where the spotter comes in, to help the lifter complete the last repetition and set the barbell safely away. On any exercise where a barbell or dumbbell might be dropped, causing physical damage, it's a good idea to use a spotter. If you're asked to spot and you aren't sure what to do, be certain to tell the person who asked that you're willing to help but that they need to tell you how they like their spotting done. As a spotter, you should always position yourself so that you can assist the lifter without getting in his or her way.

Using a Spotter for Safety

1. The spotter can help the lifter complete a repetition if he or she can no longer support the barbell.

2. The spotter can assist the lifter in returning the barbell to its rack.

3. Use a spotter for any exercise in which a barbell or dumbbell might be dropped and cause injury.

4. If you are asked to spot and don't know what do, ask the lifter for instructions before agreeing to help out.

5. Position yourself so you can assist the lifter without getting in his or her way.

How Often Should I Lift?

Many people who start lifting weights want to see immediate results, so they hit the gym every day, and then are surprised when they don't make any progress and end up with a lot of injuries. Keep in mind that you are tearing down your muscles, so they need time to heal. For that reason, you should never exercise the same set of muscles two days in a row. Unlike aerobic workouts, you don't need to lift every day or even every other day to get and maintain a good set of muscles. You do need to lift at least twice a week or you'll lose ground, but even then your workout can be a quick, twenty minute run through. For this reason, it is possible to combine weight training with your martial arts workout without taking too much time away from the rest of your life.

Finding the Right Schedule

Twice a week:

Concentrate on the major muscle groups in your thighs, chest, abdominals and biceps.

Three Times a Week:

Work the whole body plus one additional target area each workout.

Every Day:

Use a split routine so you do not work the same muscles every day.

Weight Lifting Schedule

If you find your time and energy limited, lifting weights twice a week is a good option. You won't make as much progress as quickly as you might otherwise, but it's certainly possible to find half an hour twice a week to do some lifting. If you are limited to twice a week lifting, be certain to focus on your whole body during each workout. You might want to concentrate on the major muscles groups to get the best effect. By this I mean you will want to choose the exercises that concentrate on your thigh muscles, your chest muscles, your abdominals and maybe your biceps. Don't worry so much about your shoulders or calves.

For lifters with a little more time, you might choose a three day a week workout, such as one that you do on Mondays, Wednesdays and Fridays. You would still do a full body workout, but you might add some of the smaller muscle groups as well, so that during every lift session you do thighs, chest, abs and biceps, and on Mondays you add shoulders, Wednesdays you add calves and Fridays you add hips. This can vary depending on where you'd like to see the most improvement. If arms are your concern, then concentrate on shoulders, triceps, biceps, even the wrist, and don't worry so much about calves and hips.

The only drawback to these two schedules is that you will make slower progress than someone who works out (appropriately) every day.

The alternative is to lift each day. If you lift everyday, you don't necessarily need to devote a lot of time to it. For lifters who want to do a workout every day, you simply need to remember not to work the same muscles or muscle groups on consecutive days. This is called a split routine. For instance, on Mondays you work the upper body, on Tuesdays the lower body, on Wednesdays the upper body and so forth. In this routine, you can take Sundays off, so that every Monday is upper body day, or you can continue working out every day of the week. Since lifting is a great antidote to stress, some people like to lift every day. By following a split routine, you can pay a lot more attention to your strength training than if you follow a whole body routine. Twenty minutes of working your upper body every other day is going to show results much sooner than twenty minutes of working out your whole body every other day.

Serious weight lifters swear by the split routine. They may even get very specific, such as Mondays being back day, Tuesdays being shoulder and arm day, Wednesdays being hip and butt day, and so on. Training can easily be adapted to your schedule and your goals.

Stimulating Muscle Growth

As lifters continue their routines, they are often pleased to see how quickly results are obtained. Just a month or two of working out a couple of times a week can really change how you look and feel. But frequently lifters will hit a plateau where they don't feel like they are making much progress. For people who simply want to maintain a certain fitness level, this is not a problem. In fact, many martial artists reach a lifting plateau and then are happy to stay there since their main focus is martial arts, not weight lifting. But if you want to stimulate your muscles further, or you think being stronger could improve your martial arts, then you may want to consider different ways of stimulating muscle growth and strength.

First off, however, is the warning. Never, under any circumstances, should lifters succumb to temptation and start taking anabolic steroids. Although they might promote muscle mass growth, they are illegal to use in this way, and they are very dangerous. They can cause considerable health problems, including heart problems, and they can cause altered behavior, such as aggression. It's simply not worth it.

Dangers of Steroid Use

- sterility

- cancer of the reproductive organs

- liver damage

- increased risk of heart attack

- intestinal bleeding

- high blood pressure

- low blood sugar

- acne

- thinning hair or excess hair

- unreasonable aggression and anger, known as 'roid rage

- psychosis (loss of contact with reality)

Steroids are illegal to use for weight training. Most of the supplements found in the pro shop of the gym don't do much for you either. They may be high in calories, which can add weight, but that doesn't necessarily translate into muscle mass. It's a lot less expensive to simply drink an extra glass or two of milk a day. Unless you are planning a career in body building, you don't need to worry about adding protein to your diet. Most of us get enough as it is.

So what should you do? Well, you certainly need to eat right. Not only does this help you build muscle, it helps you maintain speed and flexibility as a martial artist. Good nutrition means avoiding fats, eating plenty of fruits and vegetables, and eating grains (pasta, rice and breads) more than meat (beef, pork or poultry). Cutting out sugar and caffeine also helps you maintain a more even energy level throughout the day. Avoiding alcohol, cigarettes and other drugs also improves your health and fitness level. It is impossible to perform at optimum levels when indulging in alcohol, cigarettes or other drugs.

You need to get enough sleep to allow your muscles the opportunity to repair themselves. And you need to be careful to avoid injury during training. If you do happen to injure yourself, you want to take special care that you're healed before you start lifting again. Following these steps will help you get a better lifting workout.

Get the Most out of your Training

Avoid fats, sugar and caffeine

Eat plenty of fruits, vegetable and grains

Avoid smoking, drinking alcohol and other drugs

Get plenty of sleep

Train safely, take time to fully recover from injuries

Making Lifting More Challenging

There are also some changes you can make in your lifting workout to stimulate muscle growth. If you have been working out only twice a week, start working out at least one more day each week. If you're already working out three days a week, consider adding a few more exercises to each routine. If you're working out five or six days a week, consider cutting back for a few weeks. You may not be giving your body enough time to recuperate before making demands on it again, and this can interfere with building muscle strength.

Also, you can vary your routine as well. If you usually do just one set of an exercise, start doing two. If you already do two, try adding a third set. If you already do three or more sets, try doing one set fewer. It's surprising what works to stimulate muscle growth. Experiment with a variety of methods to discover what helps the most.

You might also vary the number of repetitions you perform. If you usually lift ten or twelve times for each set, opt for six or seven instead. This means that you'll increase the weight that you're lifting so that the last repetition is a challenge.

You might change your routine so that one or two days a week you do lighter weights with more repetitions, while on the other workout days, you lift more weight fewer times. The same holds true for sets. If you're on a Monday, Wednesday, Friday schedule, you might do only one set of repetitions for each exercise on Mondays and Fridays, while on Wednesday, you do three sets. You can even combine changing the number of reps you do with changing the number of sets you do. For instance, if you're on a Monday, Wednesday, Friday schedule, you might do lighter weights with more repetitions on Mondays and Wednesdays, doing two sets of each. On Fridays, you might do only a few repetitions with heavier weights, and do only one set of each. The variety is practically endless, and you can discover whatever combination works for you. You may find that a different solution helps you through the different plateaus that you might encounter as you continue to train.

Make your Routine More Challenging

Add an additional workout day each week.

Add a few more exercises to each workout.

Skip one day a week for a few weeks.

Add an additional set of reps for each exercise.

Lift more weight for less reps.

Do lighter weights for two workouts and heavier for the third.

The Martial Artist's Training Program

This chapter introduces the Martial Artist's Training Program. By following this plan, you can improve your strength while keeping speed and flexibility at optimum levels. The program has five parts:

- Warm-ups and Stretching

- Lifting

- Flexibility Training

- Speed Training

- Cool Down

How to Use This Program

A number of exercises will be given for each of the five parts. How to do each exercise will be explained, along with how it benefits you. Of course, you won't do every single exercise listed. In the next chapter (Chapter Four), information on tailoring the workout to the martial art you practice will be provided. Therefore, if you practice Judo, your workout will be different than if you practice Karate. What exercises should be done for each art will be identified. In Chapter Five and Six, further information on tailoring the program for your needs will be provided.

Warm-Ups and Stretching

Before you begin any exercise routine, you need to warm up and stretch. This is especially important when lifting weights, because lifting with cold muscles significantly increases the risk of strains, sprains and tears. You can keep this part of the program simple; or, if you're prone to injuries, you can increase the amount of time you spend stretching.

Although stretching is important, it should never be done with cold muscles either. You should begin every workout with a few minutes of aerobic activity. If you're at a gym, you might hop on the treadmill or the bike for a few minutes, starting slowly and then increasing the speed or difficulty. Aim for about five minutes of aerobic activity, or until you break a light sweat. Be sure to swing your arms as you do your aerobic activity to make sure your upper body gets warmed up, too. If you're at home, you can jump rope for a few minutes, or walk briskly around the house, or even climb the stairs a couple of times.

Once you've done a few minutes worth of warming up, you'll want to stretch. Stretching helps your muscles prepare for the physical activity of lifting. Always take care when stretching or you can injure yourself. Don't bounce or jerk when stretching. Move smoothly to the position you should be in and hold the stretch for about ten seconds. Then slowly release and return to your starting position. Several stretches are illustrated here; you should feel free to add stretches as needed. These stretches are also useful in martial arts training because they prepare the muscles for kicking, punching and grappling. As you stretch, think of moving from the top of your body down. This way, you won't forget to warm up your hips because you got distracted. Even if you only plan to do an upper body workout, be sure to stretch your lower body anyway, since you do use your whole body to some degree when you are lifting.

Neck Stretch

Stretch your neck in each of the four directions. Tuck your chin toward your chest until you feel the stretch. Hold this position for ten seconds. Then, hold your head to the left, tilting it as close to the shoulder as you can. Hold this position for ten seconds. Next, hold your head to the right, keeping the position for ten seconds. Lastly, look up toward the ceiling, feeling the back of your head touch your back. Hold for ten seconds. Once you have stretched in the four directions, relax and repeat two or three times.

Tuck your chin to your chest and hold for 10 seconds.

Tilt your head to your shoulder and hold for 10 seconds. Do both sides.

Shoulder Stretch

Extend your arm horizontally. Bring it across your chest until you feel the stretch in the back of your shoulder/upper arm. Hold for ten seconds, then relax and repeat. Then, arm still horizontal to the ground, reach to the back (without twisting at the waist). Hold for ten seconds, then relax and repeat. Do each stretch three or four times for each shoulder.

Extend your arm horizontally. Bring it across your chest and hold. Reach to the back and hold.

Shoulder Stretch II

Swing your arms out from the side. Then reach toward the ceiling, stretching your arms up as much as possible. Hold the stretch for ten seconds.

Reach for the ceiling and hold for ten seconds. (side view)

Reach for the ceiling and hold for ten seconds. (front view)

Arm Rotation

With both arms extended horizontally, make circles with your hands, going forward then backward. Work slowly, stretching the muscles, not bouncing them or rotating quickly. Repeat ten times in each direction.

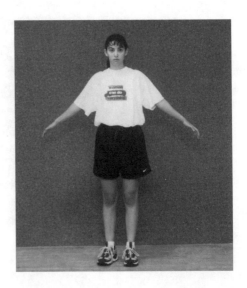

With both hands extended horizontally, make circles with your hands, first going forward and then backward.

Arm Rotation II

Swing your arms up in front of you, making a circle from front to back. Repeat 10 times in each direction.

Swing your arms in front of you, making a circle from front to back. Reverse and swing in the opposite direction. Repeat 10 times in each direction.

Wrist Stretch

To loosen your wrist and hand, extend your arm slightly in front of your body. Keeping your palm open, pull your fingers back. Hold for ten seconds. Repeat five times for each hand.

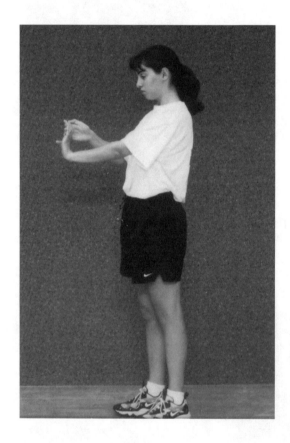

Extend your arm slightly in front of your body. Keeping your palm open, pull your fingers back and hold for 10 seconds.

Back Stretch

In a seated position, stretch your legs out in front of you. Reach forward with your hands, trying to touch the tips of your toes. Keep your legs straight--don't bend your knees. Don't overdo it and don't bounce. Hold the position for ten seconds, then relax and repeat two more times.

Stretch your legs out in front of you. Reach forward trying to touch your toes while keeping your legs straight.

Back Stretch II

Sit on the floor with your legs crossed. Keeping your body straight, gently bend toward the floor. The idea is to touch your chin to your legs, but don't overstretch. Do as much as feels comfortable. Reach your maximum stretch. (No bouncing!) Hold for ten seconds, relax and repeat. To stretch your shoulders at the same time, put your arms in front of you, bend them at the elbows, and hold them together. Then bend, touching your elbows to the floor.

Sit with your legs crossed. Gently bend to the floor keeping your body straight. Hold for 10 seconds.

Hip Flexor Stretch

The flexor muscle is on top of the hip, running from the lower abdomen to the thigh. This muscle is easily strained, so stretch it thoroughly. Kneel with one knee on the floor. The other knee should be bent at a 90 degree angle, foot flat on the floor. Slowly roll your hip forward so that you feel the stretch on top of your hip and thigh. Support yourself by placing your hands on the floor; putting hands on hips or knees causes too much stress. Hold the forward position for about ten seconds, then relax and repeat. Switch legs and repeat.

Place one knee on the floor. Slowly roll your hip forward until you feel the stretch and hold for 10 seconds.

Hip/Groin Stretch

In a seated position, extend your legs straight out in front of you. Then slide your feet toward you, bending your knees, until the soles of your feet are touching and your knees are out to the side. Continue moving your legs toward you until you feel a good stretch. Hold the position for ten seconds. Then, for a further stretch, lean forward, trying to touch your forehead to your feet. Hold this position for ten seconds. Relax and repeat.

Seated, extend your legs straight out in front of you. Slowly slide your feet toward you, until the soles of your feet are touching. Stretch forward to touch your forehead to your feet.

Hip Stretch

Stand with your palm against a wall for support. Bend your knee and rotate your leg in a circle, moving your leg out from the front to the side slowly. Then rotate your bent leg from the side back to the front. Repeat this rotation several times for both legs, moving slowly and gently at first and then moving with greater speed as you warm up the hip area.

Stand with your palm against the wall for support and lift your knee.

Rotate your leg in a circle from the front to the side and back. Repeat several times.

Hamstring Stretch

Lie on your back. Place your hands or a rolled up towel under the small of your back for support. Lift your leg up and extend it at a 90 degree angle to the floor. Continue moving your leg toward you. Keeping your leg straight, try to touch your knee to your shoulder. Don't overdo the stretch, and don't bounce. When your leg is at its full stretch, hold for ten seconds, then relax and repeat. Slowly lower your leg to the floor and stretch the other leg.

Lie on your back and extend your leg at a 90 degree angle. Keeping your leg straight, try to touch your knee to your shoulder.

Hamstring Stretch II

Sit on the floor, legs stretched out in front. Pull one knee toward your chest until you feel the stretch. Hold for ten seconds. Repeat five times for each leg.

Sit on the floor and pull one knee toward your chest. Hold for 10 seconds.

Quadriceps Stretch

Stand near a wall, putting one hand on the wall for support. Extend your leg out behind you, and bend your knee. With your free hand, reach behind and pull your ankle toward your buttocks. Hold in this position for ten seconds. Repeat five times on each leg.

Extend your leg out behind you and bend it at the knee. Pull your ankle toward your buttocks. Hold for 10 seconds.

Thigh Stretch

Lying on your stomach, place your arms under your head. (Use a mat for comfort.) Lift one leg about 12 inches off the floor. Hold for ten seconds. Relax and repeat five times on each leg.

Lying on your stomach, place your arms above your head.

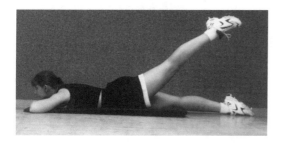

Lift one leg about 12 inches off the floor and hold for 10 seconds.

Calf Raises

Standing straight, lift your heels off the ground until you are standing on your toes. (Place your palms against a wall if you find it hard to keep your balance). Hold this stretch for ten seconds. Then lower your heels to the ground and rock back until your toes are off the ground. Hold this stretch for ten seconds. Then repeat five times.

Stand facing the wall. Hold the wall for support if you need to.

Lift your heels off the ground until you are standing on your toes. Holds for 10 seconds.

Calf Stretch

Stand facing a wall. Place your palms against the wall, about a shoulder's width apart, elbows bent slightly. Extend your leg behind you until your toes are just touching the ground. Then press down with your heel, stretching the calf muscle. Hold for about ten seconds, then relax and repeat.

Place your palms against the wall. Step behind you until your toes are just touching the ground. Press down with your heel and hold for 10 seconds.

Stance Stretches

Stance stretches stretch several main muscle groups and improve your martial arts techniques at the same time. Position yourself in any of the stances that you have been taught. Then lower your stance until you feel the stretch. Hold for about ten seconds, relax and repeat.

Some of the most common stances for stretches are the horse stance, the front stance and the back stance. The horse stance stretch is done by placing the feet parallel, about a shoulder's width apart, and bending the knees at a 90 degree angle. The front stance, also known as a forward stance, is done by placing one leg forward, bending the knee at a 90 degree angle, and keeping the back leg straight, with both feet firmly planted on the ground. The back stance is done by keeping both feet on the same line, and bearing most of your weight on the back leg, keeping the heel of the front leg off the floor.

Avoid deep stance stretches if you have knee problems.

Ankle Rotation

Sitting on the floor, prop your ankle up by crossing your legs. Rotate your ankle in all directions. Count to ten as you rotate, then reverse directions. Do five rotations with each ankle.

*Rotate your ankle
in both directions.*

These stretches are just to get you started. You may find others that you prefer, or that work better for your particular needs. But remember, proper stretching is essential. Don't overstretch and don't bounce while stretching. Never continue a stretch if you feel pain. All stretches should be done slowly and precisely. Most of all, don't forget to stretch before lifting.

Stretching Tips

1. Don't overstretch

2. Don't bounce while stretching

3. Stop if you feel pain.

4. Stretch slowly.

5. Stretch before lifting.

Strength Training Without Equipment (Isometrics)

If you don't have access to weight equipment, you can build strength by using your own body weight as resistance. You won't bulk up as much as if you used weights, but most martial artists prefer not too add to much muscle mass anyway. Crunches and push-ups are the main ways you can increase strength without needing equipment; pull ups can also be done, but you do need a pull up bar for this. Strength training without equipment is also useful for times when you don't have access to your regular weights, such as when you are traveling. By performing these exercises when weights are unavailable, you will at least be able to maintain some of your strength gains. Also, even if you regularly lift weights, these exercises are hard to duplicate in the weight room and can actually work better than weight training. For instance, doing crunches will tone your abs more effectively than using an ab machine at the gym. So to really increase your strength, add a couple of crunches and some push-ups to every lifting session. Do these right after your stretches so that you don't forget.

Crunches

Crunches work your abdominal muscles. Although sit-ups were once recommended for strengthening this area of the body, they are now considered too dangerous, because of the stress they put on your back and your neck.

To perform a basic crunch, lie on the floor, knees bent, feet on the floor. Put your hands behind your ears. Don't put your hands under your neck or lace your fingers together because this creates too much strain on your neck. Using your abdominal muscles, roll forward so that your shoulders lift off the ground. Moving slowly and deliberately, return to your starting position. You need to move slowly and smoothly to avoid using momentum instead of muscles to do the work. Repeat the crunch fifteen times.

There are a number of variations you can use (avoid these if you have back problems):

1. Twist to the right as you crunch, by leading with your left shoulder. Then twist to the left by leading with your right shoulder. This type of crunch works your oblique abdominal muscles, which are otherwise hard to tone.

2. Cross one leg over other so that the ankle of one leg rests on the thigh of the other. Perform a set of crunches, then switch legs and perform another set of crunches.

3. Extend your legs and lift them in the air 45 degrees, then perform a set of crunches. Next, raise your legs to 90 degrees as you perform each crunch. For an added degree of difficulty, cross your legs before you lift them.

Variations of Crunches

Starting position

Twist to the side

Cross one leg over

Lift your legs

Boxer Sit-ups

Boxer sit-ups are best done if you work with a partner. Lie on your back, head slightly between the feet of your partner, who should be standing. Grasp your partner's ankles and raise your legs 90 degrees. Have your partner push your legs down forcefully. Don't let them touch the ground. Lift your legs back up and have your partner push them down again. Work as quickly as possible. Repeat 15 times.

As a variation, have your partner push your legs to the right or the left instead of straight down.

If you don't have a partner, lie on your back, lift your legs up 90 degrees and then roll your hips off the ground as if you were trying to touch the ceiling with your feet. Move slowly and smoothly through the exercise without pausing. Repeat 15 times.

Push-ups

To perform a push-up, lie flat on the floor and place your palms on the floor directly under your shoulders, about a shoulder's width apart. Keeping your abdomen tight and your back and shoulders straight, push up. (Rest your knees on the floor if necessary.) Repeat fifteen times. Add push-ups in increments of five as you improve, until you can do fifty resting only your palms and toes on the floor. Knuckle push-ups, an old martial arts standby, strengthen your wrists so that they won't roll when you punch. These are done by making your hands into fists and resting your weight on the first two knuckles of each hand (your punching knuckles).

Other variations work different muscle groups. These are done by changing the placement of your hands:

1. Spread your hands so they are extended two shoulder's widths apart to work your shoulder muscles.

2. Bring your hands in close under your sternum to work your triceps.

Pull-ups

If a pull-up bar (sometimes called a chin-up) is available, work on pull-ups. If you can't do these well at first, have a partner act as spotter. (The spotter should grasp your hips and help you lift yourself up.) Grip the bar with hands about a shoulder's width apart and pull straight up. You goal should be to perform five or more without a spotter's help.

Variations work different muscle groups. These can be done by changing your grip on the bar. You can widen your grip (which works the back and triceps) or use a backward grip (which works the biceps).

Building Strength Through Martial Arts Techniques

Practicing kicks and punches full power is a time-tested way to increase strength. You'll need a heavy bag to do this, or a strong partner with a kicking target. Your goal should be to knock the heavy bag (or your partner) back at least several inches with every technique. Practice techniques in a continual motion for two minute rounds for the best workout. Avoid using axe kicks, hooking kicks, and spinning kicks at full power because the impact forces the joint against its natural range of motion; this can cause injury. Safer kicks to use are sidekicks, roundhouse kicks, and reverse kicks. You can use almost any hand or elbow striking technique as well.

If you don't have access to a heavy bag or a cooperative partner, you can still build strength through practicing martial arts techniques by slow motion kicking. This is actually a great drill even if you do have a partner and a heavy bag.

Begin by practicing your techniques slowly in front of a mirror. Tense your muscles throughout the movement (this is called *dynamic tension*), and try to perform the technique as perfectly as possible. Although you can practice hand techniques in slow motion, the real strength building comes when you practice kicks slowly. Use this time to perfect your techniques, as well. Look at your chamber. Is it high? Is it tight? Is your foot in the correct position? Is your body straight? As you get the hang of kicking slowly (it requires balance and a certain amount of practice), continually slow down your kicks until it looks as if you are practicing in slow motion. Gradually increase the amount of time it takes for you to do each kick. Aim for a goal of spending an entire sixty seconds on one technique. Practice each of your kicks in slow motion, using each of your legs ten times for an excellent strength building workout.

Using Weight Equipment

When you use weights to exercise, you need to use correct form and you need to follow a certain sequence of lifts. You should always plan your lifts so that you use the major muscle groups first before moving onto the smaller muscle groups. For example, you should perform the Leg Press, which works the thighs, hips and calves, before you perform a Hamstring Curl, which works just the hamstring. The Chest Press should be performed before the Triceps Extension is done. This prevents you from exhausting the smaller muscles before you get a chance to target them.

The correct form is slightly different for each lift, but some general rules always apply. First, you should always lift smoothly and evenly. Don't lift too quickly—that's a good way to hurt yourself. Remember that lifting and lowering a weight should take four or five seconds. Don't lock your joints when you lift. If you're doing a Leg Extension, for instance, don't straighten your leg completely until the joint is rigid. This is a sure way to injure your joints. Keep the motion smooth and even as you lift and lower the weight. Be sure to breathe as you lift, exhaling during the difficult part and inhaling through the easier part.

If you're using a machine, you should have enough control so that the weight plates don't bang together as you set them down. If you can't control the weight plates, choose a lighter weight. You should adjust the seat height and distance before using a weight machine. Be certain you understand how to work the machine before you use it.

If you're using free weights, be sure you know the proper form for each exercise. Never lift weights by bending from your waist. Always bend your knees to lift. Be careful to tighten collars on weight plates so that they don't come loose. Make sure you use a spotter whenever you are working in a position where a dropped weight could cause physical harm. Also, use a spotter when you try to lift more weight than usual, when trying out a new exercise, and when trying to do one or two more reps than usual.

Using Weight Equipment Correctly

1. Always work the major muscle groups before the smaller muscle groups.

2. Lift smoothly and evenly.

3. Each exercise should take 4 to 5 seconds.

4. Don't lock your joints.

5. Breathe as you lift.

6. Don't let the weight plates bang together.

7. Adjust the height and distance of the machine before beginning.

8. Understand how to work the machine correctly.

9. Always bend your knees to lift.

Bench Press

This exercise works the chest, triceps and the front of the shoulder.

A barbell is usually used, but dumbbells (one in each hand) can also be used. It is performed by lying on the bench with your feet flat on the floor. Grip the bar so that your hands are about a shoulder's width apart. Lift the bar straight up in line with your shoulders, straightening your arms. Then lower the bar until your elbows dip slightly below the plane of the bench. Push the bar back up to repeat the exercise.

Starting position

Bench press using dumbbells

Bench press using barbell with a spotter

Chest Press

This exercise is the same as the bench press except you use a weight machine. To perform this exercise on a machine, sit in the seat, adjusting it so that the handles are parallel to the middle of your chest. Press down on the foot pedal or plate. The handles will move toward you. Grip the handles. Slowly let go of the foot pedal. You should feel the weight of the weight stack.

Now you're ready to do the exercise. Bend your elbows and move your arms back until your hands are just an inch or two from your chest. Then push forward, straightening your arms. Slowly bend your elbows until your hands are again just an inch or two from your chest. When you're done with your set, step on the foot pedal, let go of the handles and slowly release the foot pedal to set the weight stack back down.

Sit with the handles parallel to the middle of your chest.

Push forward, straightening your arms.

Bench Fly

This exercise works the chest, the shoulders and the biceps.

Use a pair of dumbbells. Lie down on the bench, with your feet flat on the floor. Extend your arms straight up. Then, bend your elbows and move your arms to the sides, elbows pointing down. Lower your arms until your elbows move just past the plane of the bench. Keeping your elbows bent, press your arms back toward each other. Lower your arms until your elbows move just past the plane of the bench and repeat.

 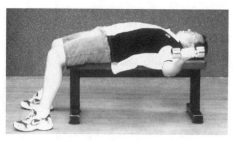

Extend your arms straight up   *Lower your arms*

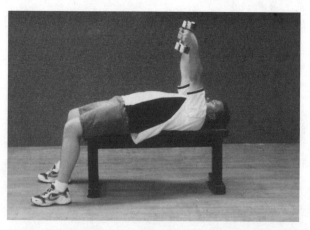

With your elbows flexed, raise your arms back toward each other

Butterfly Press

This exercise is the same as the bench fly except you use a weight machine. Sitting in the seat, reach behind you and, keeping your elbows bent so that your upper arms are parallel to the floor, place your palms and forearms flat against the padded handles. Squeeze your arms toward each other, trying to touch your palms together across your chest. When your hands are a few inches apart, spread your arms to lower the weight.

Place your palms and forearms flat against the padded handles.

Squeeze your arms together.

Military Press

This exercise works the shoulders and triceps. Using free weights, you can perform this exercise with dumbbells or a barbell. To do this exercise with dumbbells, sit on a bench, holding a pair of dumbbells. Bend your elbows so that your upper arms are parallel with the floor. Lift your arms so that your upper arms are at shoulder height. Push the dumbbells straight up over your head, then lower them back down to the starting position. To use a barbell, sit on a bench with a rack that's about shoulder high. Grip the bar with your hands about a shoulder's width apart and lift the bar off the rack. Then push straight up. Lower the bar toward your chest, just under chin height.

Starting position   *Military press with dumbbells*

Military press using barbell

Overhead Press

This exercise is the same as the military press except you use a weight machine. Adjust the seat so that to reach the handles you must bend your elbows, your upper arms parallel to the floor, at shoulder height. Grip the handles and push straight up. Then slowly lower the handles, bending your elbows, until your upper arms are about shoulder height.

Adjust the seat height so your elbows are bent to start.

Push straight up.

Lateral Pull Down

This exercise works the "laterals," the muscles that run along the side of the chest and the back. It also works the shoulders and biceps.

This exercise is usually done with a machine. To get in position for this exercise, you'll need to sit in the seat, adjusting it for height. Then stand and grab the handle above you. Sit down, gripping the bar with your hands about a shoulder's width apart. Extend your arms straight up. Now you're ready to begin the exercise. Pull the handle straight down until it is even with your chest, then slowly extend your arms straight up. When you are finished with your set, stand up, then release the handle, allowing the weight stack to return to its position.

Grip the bar with your hands shoulder width apart.

Slowly extend your arms straight up.

Lateral Raises

This exercise works the "laterals," the muscles that run along the side of the chest and the back. It also works your shoulder muscles.

It is usually done with free weights. Use a pair of dumbbells. Hold them in front of you, keeping your elbows slightly bent. Slowly swing your arms out to the sides and up to about shoulder height. Then move your arms back down to the starting position.

Start with your hands at your sides.

Raise your arms to shoulder height.

Seated Row

This exercise works the back, the back of the shoulders and the biceps. It is usually done with a weight machine. It is performed by sitting on the seat, facing the machine. Your chest should rest against the chair pad, and your arms should be fully extended. Grip the handles and pull them toward you. Your elbows should move directly back. When your hands are near your chest, slowly straighten your elbows.

Grip the handles with your arms fully extended.

Pull the handles to your chest.

Shrug

This exercise works the upper back and the shoulders. It can be done with free weights or by using a weight machine. As a free weight exercise, you can use a barbell or a pair of dumbbells.

If you use dumbbells, stand, holding the dumbbells at your sides, arms straight. Move your shoulders straight up, as if you were shrugging. Then relax your shoulders. If you use a barbell, simply hold the bar slightly in front of you, and move your shoulders straight up in a shrugging motion. If you use a weight machine, grip the bar with both hands. Lift your shoulders straight up, then relax.

Begin with shoulders relaxed

Move your shoulders straight up

Biceps Curl

This exercise works the biceps muscle of the arm. It can be done using free weights or machine weights. If you're using free weights, you can use a barbell or a pair of dumbbells.

To use dumbbells, stand with your arms extending down at your sides. Bring one arm up, bending at the elbow. Your palm should face you as you complete the movement. Then, straighten your arm back out. After you complete a set with one arm, do the same with your other arm.

To use a barbell, grip the bar so that it rests on the top of your thighs. Your hands should be about a shoulder's width apart. Bend your elbows so that the bar curls up, not quite touching your chest. Then straighten your arms so that the bar returns to its position near your thighs.

Using a machine, adjust the position of the seat so that when your arms rest on the pad, they're parallel to the floor and in line with your shoulders. Extend your arms straight out. Grip the handle. Pull the handle toward you by bending your elbow. Be sure your shoulders aren't doing the work. Then extend your arm so that it is almost straight, and repeat.

Rest the barbell on your thighs

Bend your arms.

Start position.

Pull toward you.

Triceps Extension

This exercise works the triceps muscle of the arm. It can be done using free weights or machine weights.

To use free weights, hold a pair of dumbbells in your hands. Stand straight, with your arms hanging down. Move your arm straight back as if you were reaching behind you. Reach as far back as you can. Then move your arm back to the starting position. Repeat using the other arm.

Using dumbbells, reach as far behind you as possible.

To use machine weights, sit with your upper arms parallel to the ground. Grasp the handles. Then slowly straighten your arm, pulling the weight stack up. Move your arm back to its bent position and repeat with the other arm.

Grasp the handles.

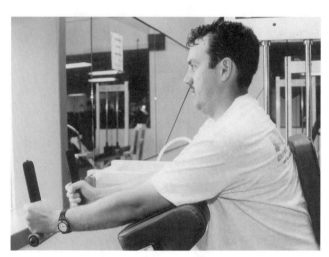

Straighten your arms, lifting the weight stack.

Abdominal Curl

This exercise works the abdominal muscles. To use the abdominal machine, adjust the seat so that the padded arm rests against your chest. Then, lean forward, using your abdominal muscles to move the weight stack as you go. Slowly return to your original position.

A good alternative is to do abdominal crunches, which are described earlier in this chapter.

Rest the padded arm against your chest.

Lean forward, using your abs to move the weights.

Hamstring Curl

This exercise works the back of the thigh. It is usually done using a weight machine. Seat yourself so that your legs extend out in front of you and your calves rest on the padded bar. Then bend your knees until they reach about a 90 degree angle. Slowly extend your legs until they are straight.

Rest your calves on the padded bar.

Bend your knees to about 90 degrees.

Squat/Leg Press

This exercise works the thighs, calves and butt. Using free weights, it is called the Squat; using machine weights it is called the Leg Press. If you're using free weights, you can use either dumbbells or a barbell.

Using a pair of dumbbells, stand straight with your arms hanging down near your sides, a dumbbell in each hand. Bend your knees as if you were about to sit in a chair. Squat as far as you can go, until your thighs are parallel to the floor. Slowly stand back up.

To do this exercise with a barbell, place the bar across your shoulders and hold it with both hands. Then, bend your knees as if you were about to sit in a chair, squatting until your thighs are parallel to the floor. Then return to a standing position.

To use the Leg Press machine, lie on your back, knees bent at a 90 degree angle, calves parallel to the floor. Position your feet firmly on the foot plate. Make sure your shoulders fit snugly against the shoulder rest. Extend your legs forward, pushing the foot plate smoothly and evenly until your legs are straight. Then bend your knees until you are back in the starting position. As a variation, place only your toes on the plate and push. This exercises your calf muscles.

Starting position for dumbbells.   *Squat as far as you can go.*

Using a barbell.   *Using a weight machine.*

Abductor Machine

This exercise works the abductor (outer thigh) muscles. It is usually done with a weight machine. Place your outer thigh against the cushioned bar. Raise your leg outward as far as possible. Then return to the starting position.

Place your outer thigh against the bar.

Raise your leg as far as possible.

Adductor Machine

This exercise works the adductor (inner thigh) muscles. It is usually done with a weight machine. Lift your leg and place it over the cushioned bar so that your inner thigh rests against the cushion. Pull your leg down and across, in front of your body. Then return to the starting position.

Place your leg over the bar.

Pull your leg down and across.

Leg Extension

This exercise works the front of the thigh (the quadriceps). It is usually done with a weight machine. Sit with your legs bent so that the top of your foot and the front of your shin cradle the padded bar. Then, holding onto the handles that are located near your hips, straighten your legs and lift the bar. Then bend your knees to return to the starting position.

Sit with your legs bent.

Straighten your legs and lift the bar.

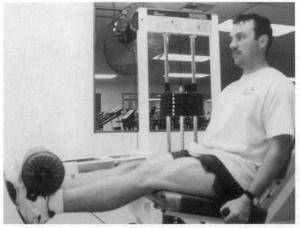

Calf Raises

This exercise works the calves. It can be done with free weights or a weight machine. If you're using free weights, you can use either dumbbells or a barbell. Using dumbbells, hold one in each hand. Stand with your feet a few inches apart, and raise your heels so that you stand on your toes. Then lower your heels. To use a barbell, place the bar across your shoulders and grip it with both hands, then raise and lower your heels.

To use the Calf Machine, stand with your shoulders under the pads and lift your heels off the ground. Then slowly lower them back to the original position.

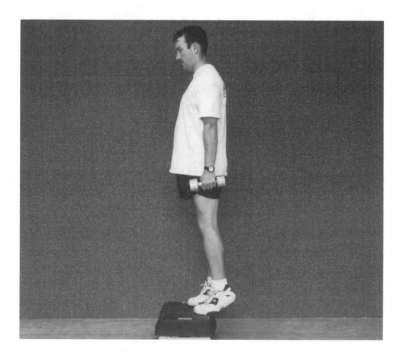

Stand with your feet a few inches apart and raise your heels.

Traditional Strength Training Methods

Some martial artists like to use traditional methods of building strength. These can also be used to spice up a standard weight lifting routine. What follows are the most common traditional methods of building strength.

Makiwara Board

In Korean martial arts, this is called the dalyeun-ju. It is simply a striking post that is used to condition the hands, and by extension, the arms. It is a thick piece of lumber with padding attached to it, which the martial artists strikes with punches or other hand techniques.

Mook Jong

This is a wooden dummy used in Wing Chun and other martial arts to increase striking and trapping skills. It is equipped with wooden arms and legs that are struck to simulate sparring with a partner. This conditions the hands and arms.

Kan Shu

This is a pail filled with abrasive material, such as sand or even gravel. The martial artist repeatedly thrusts his or her hands into this pail. The abrasive material hardens the hands.

Kame

These are jars filled with heavy materials, such as stones. They are lifted and carried to increase grip strength and arm strength.

Chashi or Sashi

This is a Chinese training device that is made from a heavy block of stone with a handle attached, much like a barbell or a dumbbell. It is used to increase strength in the wrist and forearm. It is carried while the martial artist performs a form.

Chi Shing Chung

This is a Chinese device used to strengthen legs for kicks. Several posts are placed in the ground. The martial artist kicks the posts, eventually growing strong enough to break them.

Flexibility Training

In order to avoid one of the problems associated with weight training, martial artists need to incorporate flexibility training into their weight lifting workout. This can be done after the lifts are completed, while the muscles are still warm and relaxed. Again, a number of flexibility exercises will be described, but you will only need to incorporate those that aid your martial art training. To maintain your flexibility and to prevent injury, you should do both warm-up stretches and flexibility exercises. Although they have much in common, the warm-up stretches are designed to warm-up the whole body and to get the entire body ready for a workout. The flexibility exercises are targeted at increasing the flexibility of specific joints or muscles. So the two types of exercises work together for optimum strength and flexibility without injury.

Side Bend

Standing up straight, tilt your upper body to the side, reaching over the top of your head with the opposite arm. Stretch as far as you can and hold for ten seconds. Repeat on both sides ten times.

Leg Lifts

Lying on your back, lift one leg as far off the ground as possible. Hold for fifteen seconds. Then relax and repeat, five times for each leg. Then, lift both legs off the ground at the same time, and hold for ten seconds. Relax and repeat five times.

If you have low back problems, you can lie on your side (use a mat) and, keeping your knee bent, gently bring your leg in towards your chest.

Upper Body Lift

On your stomach, push your upper body up off the floor as far as possible, keeping your hips in contact with the floor at all times. Hold the position for ten seconds and repeat five times.

Body Bridge

On your back, bend your knees so that your feet rest flat on the floor. Then, reach up toward the sides of your head and place your palms on the floor.

Arch your back as high as you can, letting your head tilt back. Hold the position for ten seconds. Then gently lower yourself to the ground and repeat five times.

Groin Stretch

Sit with your legs in front of you. Spread them in a V-shape as far apart as possible. Bend at the waist, leaning toward your left leg. Try to touch the bottom of your left foot with your hands. Hold the position for ten seconds, then relax and stretch again. Repeat five times on both sides. Then relax and, bending at the waist, lean forward between your legs, trying to stretch forward so that your chest rests on the ground. Hold this position for ten seconds, then relax and repeat five times.

Hurdle Stretch

A variation of the Groin Stretch. Keep one leg extended, but pull the other leg in so that it is bent comfortably at the knee. Try to touch the foot of the extended leg with your hands. Hold this position for ten seconds, and repeat five times on each side.

Shoulder Roll

Stand with your arms hanging straight down at your sides. Lift your shoulders up near your ears, then rotate them to the back and down. Continue making a circular movement ten times, then reverse direction and roll your shoulders the opposite way for ten counts.

Elbow Push

Cross one arm over your head. With the other hand, press your elbow toward you so that you feel the stretch in the back of your arm and shoulder. Hold for ten seconds, then repeat with the other arm.

Wrist Pull

Put your arms behind your back. Grab one wrist with the other hand. Reach behind and up with both hands until you feel the stretch in your shoulders and upper back. Hold for ten seconds then relax and repeat.

Bicycle Stretch

Lie on your back, using a mat for comfort. Slide your hands under the small of your back for support. Lift your legs in the air and move them in a circular motion, as if you were riding a bike. "Bicycle" for twenty seconds, then reverse direction and "bicycle" in the opposite direction for twenty seconds.

Hamstring Lift

Stand with your back against a wall for support. Lift one leg off the ground as if you were doing a front kick. Hold the leg in the extended position for fifteen seconds, then relax and repeat with the other leg. Try to kick and hold your leg higher with each attempt. Do five lifts with each leg. For a better stretch, have a partner hold your extended leg and push up until you feel the stretch, then hold the position while your partner slowly releases your leg.

Groin Lift

Stand with your side against the wall. Lift one leg off the ground as if you were doing a side kick. Hold the leg in the extended position for fifteen seconds, then relax and repeat with the other leg. Try to kick and hold your leg higher with each attempt. Do five lifts with each leg. To achieve a better stretch, have a partner hold your extended leg and push up until you feel the stretch, then hold the position while your partner slowly releases your leg.

Chambering Drill

To improve your flexibility and to ensure good tight chambers when you kick, stack cushions or pillows on the floor or a low bench and practice chambering your kick high enough to kick over the top of the cushions without knocking them over. Practice each of the kicks you know, adding cushions or pillows as your skill and flexibility inc eases.

Speed Training

Because weight training can sometimes slow a martial artist down, it's important to add some speed training elements to your lifting routine. The games you played as a kid are great for building speed— hopscotch, jump rope and the like are all excellent ways of building speed. So spend five minutes jumping rope in order to increase your explosive speed. If you're not inclined to jump rope, the following are a few basic speed exercises that will help you maintain and even improve your agility and quickness.

Frog Jumps

Squat on the floor, keeping your hands out for balance. Leap frog your way across the room as quickly as possible. Keep up continual leapfrogging for thirty seconds, adding on five seconds at a time. When you can do sixty leapfrogs in sixty seconds, you'll have improved your speed considerably. Do not do this drill if you have had a prior knee injury or pain in your knees while training.

Jumping Drill

Stack cushions or pillows on the floor, starting with a height of about eight inches. Jump from one side of the stack to the other as quickly as you can without stopping and without knocking the cushions over. Stack the cushions higher as you improve. When you are able to stack the cushions as high as your knees and complete fifteen jumps in thirty seconds, you'll have increased your speed considerably.

Sweeping Drill

Work with a partner for this drill. Have your partner use a blocking target (these are sold at martial arts supply houses). If a blocking target is not available, any long, flexible object will work--even the cardboard tube from a roll of wrapping paper can suffice. Have your partner sweep at your feet so that you must jump up to avoid hitting the target. Your partner should sweep back and forth quickly, without allowing pauses between jumps. Your partner can increase the height at which he or she sweeps (aiming at the knees eventually) as you improve. Once you are able to jump as high as your knees and complete twenty jumps in thirty seconds, you'll have increased your speed considerably.

Upper Body Speed Drills

If you have access to a speed bag, practicing a few minutes a day can improve the speed and timing of your hand techniques. Other speed drills that can improve the agility of your upper body and your hand and arm techniques include the following:

Punching Drill

Have a partner hold a target (or use a heavy bag). Stand so that your arm almost reaches full extension before hitting the target. Strike to the target using a hand technique, such as a punch, moving as quickly as possible. Try to return your hand to the chamber position twice as fast as you punch out with it. Use good technique. You should be able to strike about sixty times per half-minute. Build up from there. Remember to train both sides equally.

Torso Shifting Drill

To increase agility in the upper body, work with a partner. Have the partner strike at you, using different techniques, such as kicks and punches. Your partner can also use a padded target if you prefer. Keeping your feet planted, pivot at the waist and turn your upper body away from the strikes. Have your partner increase the speed with which he or she strikes and have him or her vary the height and location of the strikes. Don't move your body until your partner actually launches the strikes; then, shift out of the way as quickly as possible. Work in two-minute increments.

Cool Down

When you've finished your workout, don't just stop and sit down. Make sure you have a cooling down period. This will help prevent muscle soreness and stiffness. You can do the stretches you did at the beginning of your workout, or you can do some light walking or jogging. Some martial artists practice their techniques slowly and gently during the cool down period, working on making their form perfect instead of worrying about power and speed. Spend about five minutes cooling down from your workout and you'll help maintain your flexibility and you'll have less muscle soreness.

Training Programs for Specific Martial Arts

In Chapter Three, a workout program for martial artists is described, consisting of five parts. However, a martial artist doesn't need to do every single stretch, lift or exercise to get a good strength training workout. In fact, the program is designed so that it can be tailored to meet the needs of each specific martial art. This chapter shows you how. It features specifically designed programs for Judo/Jujutsu, Aikido, Karate and Tae Kwon Do. If the art you practice is not one of these, you can nonetheless adapt one of these programs to suit your style. For example, perhaps you practice a style that requires a lot of grappling. Then the Judo/Jujutsu workout is for you. If you practice a soft style martial art that practices blocking and using the opponent's momentum against him or her, then you'll want to choose the Aikido workout. If you practice a hard striking style that focuses on hand techniques, then you should follow the Karate workout. If your striking style emphasizes leg or kicking techniques (such as Thai boxing), then the Tae Kwon Do workout is your best bet.

The Basic Workout

Focus: Balanced full body workout

Regardless of your martial art style, you need to do a basic full body workout. Then you will add to this basic workout to target the specific needs of your style.

Warm-up

The warm-up gets your muscles ready for a workout and is an essential element of any weight training plan. It should consist of the following:

Several minutes of walking, biking, or stair climbing

Stretches

You should do a basic set of stretches in order to prepare your muscles for lifting. Proper stretching can prevent injuries. In the basic workout, you'll do stretches that focus on the large muscle groups. The specific martial art program that you use will target the smaller muscles or will focus on further stretching the large muscles and muscles groups. Basic stretches should consist of the following:

Neck Stretch (page 37)

Back Stretch (page 43)

Hip/Groin Stretch (page 46)

Hamstring Stretch (page 48)

Thigh Stretch (page 51)

Calf Raises (page 52)

Isometrics

A good strong abdominal section is necessary to perform well in all types of martial arts. Basic isometric strength training should include the following:

Crunches (page 58)

Lifts

These lifts give a basic full-body strength workout. All martial arts require a strong upper body, solid abs and a good base (hips and legs) to perform the techniques. Basic lifts should include the following:

Chest Press/Bench Press (page 68/69)

Seated Row (page 76)

Abdominal Curl (page 82) or Crunch variations (page 59)

Squat/Leg Press (page 84)

Flexibility Exercises

The basic workout includes some flexibility exercises that work the whole body. However, since most people want to maintain or increase the flexibility in their legs, that's the focus here. The following lifts help with basic flexibility for all martial artists:

Leg Lifts (page 94)

Upper Body Lift (page 95)

Groin Stretch (page 97)

Hurdle Stretch (page 98)

Speed Drills

Adding speed drills to your workout will help you train your muscles to move explosively. This means you can act and respond more quickly and more powerfully. As you build strength, you can still build speed by incorporating these drills into your program:

Frog Jumps (page 107)

Sweeping Drill (page 109)

Punching Drill (page 111)

Cool Down

Several minutes of walking, biking, or stair climbing, slowly reducing speed as you go.

Judo-Jujutsu Workout

Focus: Upper body strength + Leg strength

For grappling arts, upper body strength is of particular importance. Arm strength and grip strength are essential. Therefore, this workout emphasizes the upper body. However, since grappling styles also require throws and takedowns, some emphasis on leg strength, for hooking and breaking the opponent's balance, is also required. To the basic workout, add the following:

Stretches

You'll want to make sure you prevent injury to your arms. Because of the grappling nature of Judo/Jujutsu, shoulder problems, such as rotator cuff strains or tears, can happen. The following stretches allow you to pay particular attention to the arms and shoulders. Also, the Judo/Jujutsu practitioner must takedown or throw the opponent, and often must use pins, holds and locks. For this reason, the back, hips and hamstrings require some attention, so that those muscles don't become strained. Add the following stretches to the basic workout:

Shoulder Stretch (page 38)

Shoulder Stretch II (page 39)

Arm Rotation II (page 41)

Back Stretch II (page 44)

Hamstring Stretch (page 48)

Hip Stretch (page 47)

Isometrics

The focus on the upper body means that most strength exercises should concentrate on the arms, chest and shoulders. Therefore, you should add these isometric exercises to your basic workout:

Push-ups, with variations (page 62)

Pull ups (page 64)

Lifts

This lift routine will produce a solid upper body. The attention to lateral pulldowns and raises will aid grappling, making the trunk (chest, both sides of the chest, back) very strong. Shrugs strengthen the shoulders, which bear much of the burden in grappling. Biceps curls ensure strong arms from grabbing, pushing, pulling and holding. The hamstring curls strengthen the legs for the hooking and trapping techniques that are used against opponents while breaking their balance and throwing them.

Lateral Pulldowns (page 74)

Lateral Raises (page 75)

Shrugs (page 77)

Biceps Curls (page 78)

Hamstring Curls (page 83)

Flexibility Exercises

The Judo/Jujutsu practitioner has to maintain good upper body flexibility not only to help pin or lock an opponent but also to escape holds and pins as well. The side bend keeps the waist flexible, while the shoulder roll keeps the shoulders, arms, and upper back flexible. The wrist pull keeps the wrists supple. This joint doesn't get a lot of attention, but it helps for grabbing and holding. Keeping the upper body flexible helps the Judo or Jujutsu practitioner maintain good martial art performance. These flexibility exercises should be added to the basic workout:

Side Bend (page 93)

Body Bridges (page 96)

Shoulder Roll (page 99)

Wrist Pull (page 101)

Speed Exercises

Since the upper body requires agility in grappling arts, add this drill:

Torso Shifting Drill (page 112)

The Complete Judo/Jujutsu Workout:

Warm-up

>   Several minutes of walking, biking or stair climbing.

Stretches

>   Neck Rotation
>
>   Shoulder Stretch
>
>   Shoulder Stretch II
>
>   Back Stretch
>
>   Hip/Groin Stretch
>
>   Hamstring Stretch
>
>   Thigh Stretch
>
>   Calf Raises

Isometrics

>   Crunches
>
>   Push-ups, with variations
>
>   Pull ups

Lifts

>   Chest Press/Bench Press
>
>   Seated Row
>
>   Abdominal Curl or Crunch Variations
>
>   Squat/Leg Press

Lateral Pulldowns

Lateral Raises

Shrugs

Biceps Curls

Hamstring Curls

Flexibility Exercises

Leg Lifts

Upper Body Lift

Groin Stretch

Hurdle Stretch

Side Bend

Body Bridge

Shoulder Roll

Wrist Pull

Speed Drills

Frog Jumps

Sweeping Drill

Punching Drill

Torso Shifting Drill

Cool Down

Several minutes of walking, biking, or stair climbing, slowly reducing speed.

Variations of the Judo/Jujutsu Workout

- If you are just getting started with weight training, start with the basic workout, and slowly add the Judo/Jujutsu exercises over time.

- Instead of doing all the exercises in one workout, try splitting the workout so that you lift one day and do flexibility and speed training the next. You should warm-up and stretch and cool down at every training session.

Aikido Workout

Focus: Upper body balance, Strength+ Flexibility

Aikido requires balance in the upper body, for blocking and for circular countering movements. For this, strong arms, strong shoulders and a strong back are essential. To the basic workout, add the following:

Stretches

Since most of the Aikido techniques require upper body agility, it's important to stretch those muscles well. In addition, since a strong back and hips are needed to perform the techniques correctly, some attention should be paid to those areas as well. Add these stretches to the basic workout:

Shoulder Stretch (page 38)

Shoulder Stretch II (page 39)

Arm Rotation II (page 41)

Wrist Stretch (page 42)

Back Stretch II (page 44)

Hip Stretch (page 47)

Isometrics

The focus on the upper body means that most strength exercises should concentrate on the arms, chest and shoulders. Therefore, you should add these isometric exercises to your basic workout:

Push-ups, with variations (page 62)

Pull-ups (page 64)

Lifts

Since the Aikido practitioner does most techniques as blocking, sweeping or circular movements, arms and shoulders must be exceptionally strong. Shrugs work the shoulders and upper back, adding power to the upper body. The overhead press creates strong shoulders, for pushing and blocking movements. The lateral pulldown creates a strong trunk for pulling and trapping. Biceps curls and triceps extensions work both sides of the upper arm, creating solid arms that can block, sweep or trap an opponent. Add these lifts to the basic workout:

Shrugs (page 77)

Overhead Press (page 73)

Lateral Pulldown (page 74)

Biceps Curl (page 78)

Triceps Extension (page 80)

Flexibility Exercises

Because so many of Aikido's techniques rely on redirecting the opponent's energy and avoiding the opponent's strikes, agility and flexibility, especially in the upper body, are a must. Side bends keep the waist area supple so that it is easy to turn out of the way. Shoulder rolls and elbow pushes keep the shoulders and arms flexible. The wrist pull keeps the wrist flexible for grabbing and guiding the opponent.

Side Bend (page 93)

Shoulder Roll (page 99)

Elbow Push (page 100)

Wrist Pull (page 101)

Speed Exercises

In order to increase agility in the upper body, add the following speed drill:

Torso Shifting Drill (page 112)

The Complete Aikido Workout

Warm-up

Several minutes of walking, biking or stair climbing.

Stretches

Neck Rotation

Back Stretch

Hip/Groin Stretch

Hamstring Stretch

Thigh Stretch

Calf Raises

Shoulder Stretch

Shoulder Stretch II

Arm Rotation II

Wrist Stretch

Back Stretch

Hip Stretch

Isometrics

Crunches

Push-ups with variations

Pull ups

Lifts

Chest Press/Bench Press

Seated Row

Abdominal Curl or Crunch Variations

Squat/Leg Press

Overhead Press

Shrug

Lateral Pulldown

Biceps Curl

Triceps Extension

Flexibility Exercises

Leg Lifts

Upper Body Lift

Groin Stretch

Hurdle Stretch

Side Bend

Shoulder Roll

Elbow Push

Wrist Pull

Speed Drills

> Frog Jumps
>
> Sweeping Drill
>
> Punching Drill
>
> Torso Shifting Drill

Cool Down

Several minutes of walking, biking, or stair climbing, slowly reducing speed.

Variations of the Aikido Workout

- If you are just getting started with weight training, start with the basic workout, and slowly add the Aikido exercises over time.

- Instead of doing all the exercises in one workout, try splitting the workout so that you lift one day and do flexibility and speed training the next. You should warm-up and stretch and cool down at every training session.

Karate Workout

Focus: Arm + Leg strength

Although there are many styles of Karate, each teaching different techniques, all are hard striking styles. Therefore, the most useful exercises are those that require powerful pushing movements. Since most Karate styles also emphasize hand techniques, strength training should focus on strong arms. However, since kicks, especially middle kicks, are also used, some attention must be paid to leg strength. To the basic workout, add the following:

Stretches

In order to produce powerful arm and hand strikes, the arms and shoulders must be prepared. But because the whole body should be used to deliver a blow, the back needs to be strong, as well. Some kicks are used, so the legs should be worked. Since all Karate styles teach basic stances, one of the best ways to stretch leg muscles is to perform stance stretches. To the basic workout, these stretches should be added for Karate practitioners:

Shoulder Stretch (page 38)

Arm Rotation II (page 41)

Wrist Stretch (page 42)

Back Stretch II (page 44)

Calf Stretch (page 53)

Stance Stretches (page 54)

Isometrics

Because the upper body needs to be strong, add the following isometric strength training exercises:

Push-ups, with variations (page 62)

Pull-ups (page 64)

Lifts

In order to perform powerful strikes, lifts should focus on building muscles that push. The overhead press works shoulders, the lateral raises work arms and upper back and the butterfly press works the chest and arms. The triceps extension also works the arm muscles that push or strike. All of these lifts create a strong upper body designed for striking. Leg extensions mimic the movement needed for front kicks and middle kicks, thus rounding out the Karate workout. Add these lifts to the basic workout:

Overhead Press (page 73)

Lateral Raises (page 75)

Butterfly Press/Bench Fly (page 70/71)

Triceps Extension (page 80)

Leg Extension (page 88)

Flexibility Exercises

Keeping the wrists flexible helps the Karate practitioner perform all the different hand striking techniques in his or her arsenal. The hamstring lift, groin lift and chambering drill all help improve leg flexibility and kicking skills.

Wrist Pull (page 101)

Hamstring Lift (page 103)

Groin Lift (page 104)

Chambering Drill (page 105)

Speed Exercises

To maintain and even increase leg speed needed for kicks, add the following speed drill:

Jumping Drill (page 108)

The Complete Karate Workout

Warm-up

    Several minutes of walking, biking or stair climbing.

Stretches

    Neck Rotation

    Back Stretch

    Hip/Groin Stretch

    Hamstring Stretch

    Thigh Stretch

    Calf Raises

    Shoulder Stretch

    Arm Rotation II

    Wrist Stretch

    Back Stretch II

    Calf Stretch

    Stance Stretches

Isometrics

    Crunches

    Push-ups, with variations

    Pull-ups

*Lift*s

    Chest Press/Bench Press

    Seated Row

    Abdominal Curl or Crunch Variations

    Squat/Leg Press

    Overhead Press

    Lateral Raises

    Butterfly Press/Bench Fly

    Triceps Extension

    Leg Extension

Flexibility Exercises

    Leg Lifts

    Upper Body Lift

    Groin Stretch

    Hurdle Stretch

    Wrist Pull

    Hamstring Lift

    Groin Lift

    Chambering Drill

Speed Drills

      Frog Jumps

      Sweeping Drill

      Punching Drill

      Jumping Drill

Cool Down

Several minutes of walking, biking, or stair climbing, slowly reducing speed.

Variations of the Karate Workout

- If you are just getting started with weight training, start with the basic workout, and slowly add the Karate exercises over time.

- Instead of doing all the exercises in one workout, try splitting the workout so that you lift one day and do flexibility and speed training the next. You should warm-up and stretch and cool down at every training session.

Taekwondo Workout

Focus: Leg strength + Flexibility

Tae Kwon Do is a martial art that emphasizes striking techniques. The art relies mainly on kicks, especially high kicks and jumping kicks. For this reason, strong, flexible legs and hips are essential to good performance. To the basic workout, add the following:

Stretches

Because the legs get such a workout in Tae Kwon Do, stretching the lower body is important. Not only do the legs need attention, but the hips and groin should be stretched in order to avoid some common injuries for Tae Kwon Do practitioners. To the basic workout, add these stretches:

Hip Flexor Stretch (page 45)

Hamstring Stretch II (page 49)

Quadriceps Stretch (page 50)

Calf Stretch (page 53)

Stance Stretches (page 54)

Ankle Rotation (page 55)

Isometrics

A strong abdominal area is essential for a Tae Kwon Do practitioner, because all the kicking requires a solid base. To the basic workout, add this isometric strength training exercise:

Boxer Sit-ups (page 60)

Lifts

Because of the emphasis on kicking, strong legs are essential. Leg extensions and hamstring curls create powerful, balanced leg muscles. Calf raises provide the support necessary for pivoting and balancing on one leg. Abductor and adductor exercises work the inner and outer thighs and the hips so kicks can go higher and be stronger. Add these lifts to the basic workout:

Leg Extension (page 88)

Hamstring Curl (page 83)

Calf Raises (page 89)

Abductor Machine (page 86)

Adductor Machine (page 87)

Flexibility Exercises

To kick high, the Tae Kwon Do practitioner must have extremely flexible legs and hips. The bicycle stretch keeps the hips flexible, while the hamstring lift, groin lift and chambering drill all work to keep the legs flexible. Add these flexibility exercises to the basic workout:

Bicycle Stretch (page 102)

Hamstring Lift (page 103)

Groin Lift (page 104)

Chambering Drill (page 105)

Speed Exercises

To maintain and improve leg speed for kicking techniques, add the following speed drill:

Jumping Drill (page 108)

The Complete Tae Kwon Do Workout

Warm-up

Several minutes of walking, biking or stair climbing.

Stretches

Neck Rotation

Back Stretch

Hip/Groin Stretch

Hamstring Stretch

Hamstring Stretch II

Thigh Stretch

Quadriceps Stretch

Calf Raises

Calf Stretch

Hip Flexor Stretch

Stance Stretches

Ankle Rotation

Isometrics

Crunches

Boxer Sit-ups

Lifts

Chest Press/Bench Press

Seated Row

Abdominal Curls or Crunch Variations

Squat/Leg Press

Leg Extension

Hamstring Curl

Calf Raises

Abductor Machine

Adductor Machine

Flexibility Exercises

Leg Lifts

Upper Body Lift

Groin Stretch

Hurdle Stretch

Bicycle Stretch

Hamstring Lift

Groin Lift

Chambering Drill

Speed Drills

> Frog Jumps
>
> Punching Drill
>
> Sweeping Drill
>
> Jumping Drill

Cool Down

Several minutes of walking, biking, or stair climbing, slowly reducing speed.

Variations of the Tae Kwon Do Workout

- If you are just getting started with weight training, start with the basic workout, and slowly add the Tae Kwon Do exercises over time.

- Instead of doing all the exercises in one workout, try splitting the workout so that you lift one day and do flexibility and speed training the next. You should warm-up and stretch and cool down at every training session.

Training for Body Conditioning

Although the martial artist's workout can be tailored to meet the needs of a specific martial art, sometimes a martial artist feels the need to work on a specific aspect of conditioning, such as power, flexibility or endurance. The workout can be adjusted to meet these needs as well.

Power Plan

Focus: Strength + Speed

The power plan emphasizes weight lifting and speed training. This is because power is produced by a combination of mass and speed. For the power plan, you'll need to double the amount of time you devote to speed training. And when you lift, you'll want to max out after six or seven repetitions. This means you'll be lifting much heavier weights. You should also plan to do at least two sets of each lift during each workout to build mass more quickly.

Warm-up

Several minutes of walking, biking or stair climbing

Stretches

Do a basic set of stretches that hit all the major muscles groups in the body.

Neck Stretch (page 37)

Arm Rotation (page 40)

Back Stretch (page 43)

Hip/Groin Stretch (page 46)

Thigh Stretch (page 51)

Isometrics

Crunches, with variations (page 59)

Boxer Sit-ups (page 60)

Push-ups, with variations (page 62)

Pull ups (page 64)

Lifts

Remember to lift no more than six or seven repetitions. The weight should be heavy enough that the last repetition leads to muscle failure—that is, the muscle should be unable to lift again without resting for at least a few seconds. After six weeks or so, you can really build strength by continuing to reduce the number of repetitions you do while increasing the amount of weight you lift. Be certain to give yourself enough recovery time between lifts, either by lifting every other day or by following a split lift routine where you work the upper body one day and the lower body the next.

Chest Press/Bench Press (page 68/69)

Butterfly Press/Bench Fly (page 70/71)

Overhead Press/Military Press (page 73/72)

Lateral Pulldown (page 74)

Lateral Raise (page 75)

Seated Row (page 76)

Shrug (page 77)

Biceps Curl (page 78)

Triceps Extension (page 80/81)

Squat/Leg Press (page 84)

Hamstring Curls (page 83)

Leg Extension (page 88)

Calf Raises (page 89)

Speed Training

Remember, you should devote twice as much time to speed training as in the basic workout.

Frog Jumps (page 107)

Jumping Drill (page 108)

Sweeping Drill (page 109)

Punching Drill (page 111)

Torso Shifting Drill (page 112)

Cool Down

Several minutes of walking, biking, or stair climbing, slowly reducing speed.

The Flexibility Plan

Focus: Strength + Flexibility

Because many martial artists are concerned that weight training will interfere with their flexibility, some will want to choose this option, which emphasizes flexibility while still building strength.·

Warm-up

Several minutes of walking, biking or stair climbing.

Stretches

You can start improving flexibility by paying careful attention to stretches. By stretching all the muscles, you can prepare them for a workout and for flexibility training. In fact, simply by performing stretches correctly, you can actually increase your muscle flexibility. Make sure to do these stretches:

Shoulder Stretch (page 38)

Arm Rotation (page 40)

Back Stretch (page 43)

Back Stretch II (page 44)

Hip Flexor Stretch (page 45)

Isometrics

For support during flexibility and strength training, solid abs are essential. To add balance, include push-ups.

Lifts

To improve strength without adding too much muscle mass (which can interfere with flexibility) plan your lifts so that you complete about 15 reps. The last repetition should be difficult; otherwise the weight is too light.

Chest Press/Bench Press (page 68/69)

Seated Row (page 76)

Shrug (page 77)

Squat/Leg Press (page 84)

Abductor Machine (page 86)

Adductor Machine (page 87)

Hamstring Curl (page 83)

Leg Extension (page 88)

Flexibility Exercises

Since flexibility is an essential part of this program, particular attention should be made to performing flexibility exercises correctly. Even on days that you don't lift, flexibility exercises should be done.

Side Bend (page 93)

Leg Lifts (page 94)

Upper Body Lift (page 95)

Groin Stretch (page 97)

Hurdle Stretch (page 98)

Shoulder Roll (page 99)

Elbow Push (page 100)

Wrist Pull (page 101)

Bicycle Stretch (page 102)

Hamstring Lift (page 103)

Groin Lift (page 104)

Cool Down

Several minutes of walking, biking, or stair climbing, slowly reducing speed.

The Endurance Plan

Focus: Strength + Muscular endurance

This plan is ideal for martial artists who want to improve their muscle endurance, so that sparring matches, forms, and other aspects of the martial arts are easier to perform successfully. Cardiovascular endurance requires aerobic training; for this, you will need to add about a half hour of aerobic exercise to your routine at least three times a week. This can be brisk walking, jogging, or an aerobics class.

The endurance this plan will emphasize, however, is muscle endurance, not cardiovascular endurance. Muscle endurance helps you perform even at high speed, using much of your strength, for a longer period of time. That's why training for muscle endurance is necessary for martial artists who spar, or who want to perfect their forms, or who want to improve their basic conditioning.

Warm-up

Several minutes of walking, biking or stair climbing.

Stretches

Your goal with stretches should be to hit all the main muscle groups so that you don't injure yourself lifting.

Shoulder Stretch (page 38)

Arm Rotation II (page 41)

Back Stretch (page 43)

Hip/Groin Stretch (page 46)

Thigh Stretch (page 51)

Isometrics

In order to build muscle endurance, start with working on isometric strength training. Try to build on these exercises so that you can do fifty or seventy five of them without pausing. This creates excellent muscle endurance.

Crunches, with variations (page 59)

Boxer Sit-ups (page 60)

Push-ups, with variations (page 62)

Lifts

For muscle endurance, you want to perform a wide variety of lifts. You also need to lift enough weight so that the number of repetitions you do falls into the ten-to-twelve range. This is ideal for building muscle endurance. If you do fewer reps, you'll create bigger muscles, and they'll be able to lift more, but they won't be able to work longer, which is what your goal should be for endurance training. Lifting for more reps won't challenge your muscles enough for endurance training.

Chest Press/Bench Press (page 68/69)

Butterfly Press/Bench Fly (page 70/71)

Overhead Press/Military Press (page 72/73)

Lateral Pulldown (page 74)

Lateral Raise (page 75)

Seated Row (page 76)

Shrug (page 77)

Biceps Curl (page 78)

Triceps Extension (page 80)

Squat/Leg Press (page 84)

Hamstring Curl (page 83)

Leg Extension (page 88)

Calf Raises (page 89)

Flexibility Exercises

For the endurance plan, you should do a few basic flexibility exercises because muscle endurance isn't that helpful if you don't have good flexibility.

Leg Lifts (page 94)

Upper Body Lift (page 95)

Groin Stretch (page 97)

Shoulder Roll (page 99)

Bicycle Stretch (page 102)

Speed Drills

Speed drills help train for muscle endurance since these exercises quickly exhaust the muscles. By performing these exercises repeatedly, you can build up the number of repetitions you do or the amount of time you spend doing it.

Frog Jumps (page 107)

Jumping Drill (page 108)

Sweeping Drill (page 109)

Cool Down

Several minutes of walking, biking, or stair climbing, slowly reducing speed.

Combination Workouts

If you have the goal of becoming more powerful while improving your muscle endurance, you may wonder how you can do this. Each plan requires a different strategy, so what should you do? There are several different approaches you can take. A common approach used by weight lifters is to alter their routine every month. Therefore, for one month, you might work on endurance. The next month you might work on power. You can even add in flexibility so that you are on a three month cycle. This approach helps keep your workout interesting.

Another possibility is to change the routine slightly to accommodate your goals. For example, perhaps you want to lift for power, but you don't want to sacrifice flexibility. You could continue lifting for power while adding flexibility exercises to the routine. The only drawback to this approach is that it increases the amount of time you need to complete your routine.

To overcome this drawback, you might reduce the amount of time you spend on other aspects of the power plan, such as speed. Instead of spending twice as much time on speed training, limit it to a few minutes during each workout, and add a few minutes of flexibility training to your routine.

See Chapter Six for further information on customizing your weight training program.

Customizing your Weight Training

This chapter will describe how to completely customize your own weight training workout to meet your goals and needs.

Where to Begin

If you've never lifted before, you should probably start with the basic workout described in Chapter Four for a few weeks. Once you have a sense of how the exercises and lifts are done and are comfortable with them, you can begin arranging your own program. Don't be afraid to experiment with your routine, by adding and subtracting and changing, but try not to make changes every single time you work out. This can make it difficult for your body to gain any benefit from your workout.

All workouts should have a warm-up period and a cool down period. This reduces the amount of stress you put on your body, the risk of injuries and the amount of muscle soreness you have to put up with.

Identify Your Goals

The customized program you design for yourself will depend largely on what your goals are. Therefore you should identify these goals first.

- If you want to increase power, follow the Power Plan in Chapter Five.

- If you want to increase flexibility, follow the Flexibility Plan in Chapter Five.

- If you want to increase muscle endurance, follow the Endurance Plan in Chapter Five.

- If you want to increase upper body strength, follow the Judo/Jujutsu Plan in Chapter Four.

- If you want to increase upper body flexibility and agility, follow the Aikido Plan in Chapter Four.

- If you want to increase lower body strength, follow the Tae Kwon Do Plan in Chapter Four.

If these plans don't quite fit your needs, you may want to develop one of your own. Ask yourself these questions:

• *Do I need more work on my upper body or my lower body? Or do they need equal amounts of work?*

  If so, concentrate your lifting so you can work the area that needs it. By focusing your attention, you'll minimize the amount of time you spend at the gym.

• *Am I afraid of losing flexibility and speed?*

  If so, be certain to include flexibility exercises and speed drills into your lifting program.

• *Do I want huge muscles, or do I want toned, well-defined muscles?*

  Remember, if you want big muscles, lift a lot of weight for a few reps. Otherwise, stick to lighter weights and more reps.

• *How much time do I have to devote to weight training?*

  Be realistic about how much you can accomplish. If you have a number of goals and a limited amount of time, set up a program that allows you to work on one goal at a time.

- *Have I done weight training in the past (or am I doing it now)?*

  If so, evaluate what worked in the past, what didn't work, and why. Also ask how your goals have changed over time.

- *What do I want to achieve by weight training?*

  You should identify specific goals, such as a stronger back, more powerful legs, and the like. Then you can work on building them.

- *Do I suffer from muscle or joint soreness when I exercise?*

  If so, ask yourself if it's just general soreness that comes from a workout or if it is more likely an injury. Basic muscle soreness can be overcome by gradually working into a program over a period of time and by being careful to warm-up, stretch and cool down as a part of every workout session. Injuries need to be treated carefully. (See Chapter Seven). If you've injured a joint or muscle in the past and don't want to repeat the experience, use caution when lifting.

- *Do I have difficulty performing any of the martial arts techniques I practice?*

  For instance, in Karate, you may have trouble punching quickly enough. In Aikido, you may have trouble shifting your body out of the way of strikes. In Tae Kwon Do, you might have difficulty performing a jump front kick. If so, make a list of problem areas. Then, ask yourself if any of the difficult techniques have something in common. As an example, you may have trouble doing *all* the jumping kicks, not just the jump front kick. Once you have a sense of the areas   that need work, determine what would solve the problem. As a general rule of thumb, martial arts practitioners need speed, flexibility and strength. Without one of these, your practice will lack balance, and there will be some things that are difficult to do. In the examples above, the Karate student would need to work on speed training, the Aikido student would need to work on flexibility and the Tae Kwon Do student would need to work on strength.

Building Your Program

Once you have a general sense of what your goals are, you can begin planning your own customized program. Remember that how you lift is as important as the lifts you do. If you want to build muscle mass and power, lift heavier weights for fewer repetitions (about six to eight repetitions). If you want to build muscle endurance and strength without massive muscles, lift moderate weight for more repetitions (in the ten-to-twelve range). If you want to tone and strengthen without interfering with flexibility or speed, lift lighter weights for a greater number of repetitions (about fifteen repetitions).

Select stretches, lifts and other exercises from the following guide. Remember to include some exercises of each type: *stretches, isometrics, lifts, flexibility exercises* and *speed drills*.

Upper Body Flexibility

(see also Arm/Shoulder Flexibility)

Stretches:

Neck Stretch (page 37)

Shoulder Stretch (page 38)

Arm Rotation (page 40)

Back Stretch (page 43)

Back Stretch II (page 44)

Flexibility Exercises:

Side Bend (page 93)

Upper Body Lift (page 95)

Body Bridge (page 96)

Speed Exercises:

Torso Shifting Drill (page 112)

Upper Body Strength

(see also Arm/Shoulder Strength)

Lifts:

Chest Press/Bench Press (page 68/69)

Butterfly Press/Bench Fly (page 70/71)

Lateral Pulldown (page 74)

Lateral Raise (page 75)

Seated Row (page 76)

Shrug (page 77)

Arm/Shoulder Flexibility

(see also Upper Body Flexibility)

Stretches:

Shoulder Stretch II (page 39)

Arm Rotation II (page 41)

Wrist Stretch (page 42)

Flexibility Exercises:

Shoulder Roll (page 99)

Elbow Push (page 100)

Wrist Pull (page 101)

Speed Exercises:

Punching Drill (page 111)

Arm/Shoulder Strength

(see also Upper Body Strength)

Isometrics:

Push-ups, with variations (page 62)

Pull ups (page 64)

Lifts:

Overhead Press/Military Press (page 72/73)

Biceps Curl (page 78)

Triceps Extension (page 80)

Abdominal Strength

Isometrics:

Crunches, with variations (page 59)

Boxer Sit-ups (page 60)

Lifts:

Abdominal Curl (page 82)

Lower Body Flexibility

(see also Leg Flexibility)

Stretches:

Hip Flexor Stretch (page 45)

Hip/Groin Stretch (page 46)

Hip Stretch (page 47)

Stance Stretches (page 54)

Flexibility Exercises:

Groin Stretch (page 97)

Hurdle Stretch (page 98)

Bicycle Stretch (page 102)

Lower Body Strength

(see also Leg Strength)

Lifts:

Squat/Leg Press (page 84)

Abductor Machine (page 86)

Adductor Machine (page 87)

Speed Exercises:

Jumping Drill (page 108)

Frog Jumps (page 107)

Leg Flexibility

(see also Lower Body Flexibility)

> Stretches:

Hamstring Stretch (page 48)

Hamstring Stretch II (page 49)

Quadriceps Stretch (page 50)

Thigh Stretch (page 51)

Calf Raises (page 52)

Calf Stretch (page 53)

Ankle Rotation (page 55)

> Flexibility Exercises:

Leg Lifts (page 94)

Hamstring Lift (page 103)

Groin Lift (page 104)

Chambering Drill (page 105)

Leg Strength

(see also Lower Body Strength)

Lifts:

Hamstring Curl (page 83)

Leg Extension (page 88)

Calf Raises (page 89)

Overall Speed

Frog Jumps (page 107)

Sweeping Drill (page 109)

Torso Shifting Drill (page 112)

Injury Prevention

Of course, your weight training goals won't be met if you injure yourself while training. Therefore, you will want to be careful not to hurt yourself during any part of the weight training routine. Be sure to perform all of the exercises and lifts correctly. Never bounce while performing any of these moves. Always use a smooth, even effort. If you feel pain, stop what you're doing immediately. When lifting, pay attention to good form. Remember to breathe as you lift, exhaling during the exertion phase and inhaling during the less strenuous part of the exercise.

Remember to start training gradually and to add weight and other elements to your workout schedule slowly, over a period of time. Don't overdo the intensity of your training. Most martial artists agree that working out every day is what keeps them at their peak. However, you should allow a day or two off each week to give your body a break and to let it recuperate from the small tears, aches, pains, and strains that accumulate over time. Remember to be realistic. You may find your body can do more than you ever imagined, but try not to get frustrated if it doesn't respond as quickly as you would like.

Because weight lifting doesn't seem as likely to cause injury as other physical activities, lifters sometimes overlook the amount of stress lifting can put on their bodies. It's easy to get injured without realizing it.

But most lifting injuries can be prevented. Starting slowly and building up to a level of exercise that keeps you fit is the best way to prevent typical injuries.

Injury Prevention

Although most martial artists talk about injuries as if they were inevitable, being sensible can prevent some of the most common injuries. Warming up, stretching, and cooling down are essential to avoiding injuries. Overall, the most common injuries in martial arts practice and in weight training are overuse injuries, hyperextension injuries, and sprains and strains.

Overuse Injuries

Overuse injuries, especially for beginners or for those who are training hard, can be debilitating. Overuse injuries occur when a joint is used repetitively, especially if the joint has not been used extensively before. Overuse injuries like tendinitis and bursitis can cause pain and discomfort in a joint such as a shoulder, when an individual begins using the joint more than usual. To prevent this, stretch before working out. Also, be certain to execute the lifts precisely. If you don't lift correctly, you'll put undue stress on your joints, which can cause strains, overuse injuries, and ligament damage.

Overuse injuries can be painful and can cause frustration, but they rarely cause more than temporary discomfort. If you suspect you have an overuse injury, check with your physician. Visiting with a sports medicine specialist or even a sports trainer can help you to learn how to prevent such problems.

Usually rest, ice, and an antiinflammatory such as ibuprofen (or in more extreme cases, a prescription medication) will take care of the problem. If not, an injection of cortisone and/or physical therapy may be recommended. Although overuse injuries heal, it's better for your body if you prevent injuries rather than treat them.

While all joints can be affected, for martial artists hips and knees are most commonly overused, followed by the shoulder. Why shoulders? Since martial arts advocate a variety of hand, elbow and arm techniques, one's shoulders are stressed and strained differently from usual. Since the muscle mass is usually not as well-developed here as in other parts of the body, these stresses and strains are more likely to cause an injury, especially an overuse injury. Overuse injuries include bursitis, tendinitis, plus strains, tears and stress fractures. Remember to stretch all of your joints—including your shoulders—before you start training.

Hyperextension Injuries

Hyperextension occurs when a joint is forced to move beyond its usual stopping point. This can happen when a lifter locks a joint out when lifting. It can also happen when a lifter tries to lift a weight that is too heavy or tries to lift weights too quickly. To prevent hyperextension, always keep the joint slightly relaxed. Never fully extend a joint when lifting.

Hyperextension is easily identified. If you suddenly have pain in a joint after you do a lift, and the pain persists whenever you use the affected limb, you may have hyperextended a joint. Rest, ice, anti-inflammatories—and, if pain continues or worsens—a visit to the doctor are all called for.

Acute Injuries

Sprains, strains and tears are all very similar in origin and effect. While overuse injuries have to do with using a joint or limb too much over the course of a certain amount of time—they are cumulative, in effect—strains, sprains, and tears are all usually the result of an acute injury. That is, a single event that happens suddenly and causes an injury. Perhaps you land wrong on your foot, roll your ankle and end up with a sprain. Or you attempt to improve your flexibility and suddenly you've got a tear in your hamstring. Sprains and strains can range from mild to severe. The milder cases require little attention, usually just some aspirin and some ice. More serious cases require rest, ice, compression and elevation, a treatment also known by its acronym "RICE."

1) Strain

A pulled muscle or muscle strain is usually the result of a specific injury, with pain, tenderness and swelling the usual signs. If the muscle doesn't seem to work at all, seek treatment immediately— the muscle itself may have ruptured, in which case, surgery may be necessary to repair it.

A muscle strain happens when a muscle is overstretched or overworked. The muscle continues to function—it just becomes sore. More serious strains may result in muscle tears, which require more time and rest to heal. In martial arts, the most common strains occur in the hamstring and the groin area. Most strains are quick to mend. The area should be iced on and off for 24 hours (not more than 20 minutes at one time), then a heating pad can be used. Some people prefer to ice a strained muscle the entire time it is injured. A few days of rest is usually all that is needed. More serious strains may benefit from an antiinflammatory or muscle relaxant. For this, consult your physician. To prevent such strains, be certain to warm up and stretch before working out.

Treating Injuries with RICE

If you have an acute injury such as a sprain or a strain, you should treat the injury using the "RICE" method, which medical professionals recommend.

R Rest the affected area to prevent further damage to the muscles, tendons or ligaments.

I Ice the affected area to help reduce swelling and pain. Wrap ice or an ice pack in a towel (to prevent frostbite) and apply to the injured area for fifteen minutes each hour.

C Compress the injured area to decrease swelling and prevent further injury. An injured limb or joint can be unstable. Use a compression or elastic bandage, such as an Ace bandage, to keep the area from moving.

E Elevate the affected area to prevent blood from pooling in the limb and to reduce swelling. If possible, the affected area should be elevated above the heart.

2) Sprain

A sprain, a word that is often used to identify what is actually a strain or pull, is in fact an injury to the ligaments that connect muscles to bones. Usually a twist, a misstep or an extreme stretch puts too much strain on the ligaments, and tissue is torn. The ankles, knees and even the arches of the feet are the most common areas to sustain a sprain. Rapid swelling, reduced ability to use the affected area and pain all signal a sprain. If you actually hear a snapping sound, seek treatment immediately, stopping only to apply ice to the area and to immobilize it. This snapping sound may indicate a detached ligament. (The ligament is torn from the bone and pops away, resulting in a snapping sound.) Surgery is sometimes needed to repair the damage.

For routine sprains, ice, compression and rest will cure the condition. The sprained part can usually bear weight after a day or two, but remember this doesn't mean it is completely healed. For a few weeks, minimize your workout intensity to avoid exacerbating the sprain. If the sprain is severe or the joint is unstable, the area may need to be immobilized with a cast or splint.

Physical therapy can help you regain a full range of motion. If you repeatedly sprain a certain joint, use a brace, wrap or tape to help support the area and prevent progressive weakening of and even eventual destruction of the joint. Also, consult your physician, who can recommend a sports trainer or a physical therapist for tips on preventing recurring injuries.

3) Cramps

Muscle cramps, while not exactly an injury, often occur, causing pain and discomfort for the martial artist. Sudden sharp pain or lumps of muscle tissue that can be seen or felt indicate a muscle cramp. These can happen when the muscle is injured or overused. Fatigue and dehydration can contribute to cramps. Usually, muscle cramps are just an inconvenience that will go away without special treatment. If they occur frequently or interfere with your sleep, consult your doctor. Sometimes a compressed nerve will cause muscle cramps, as will potassium loss, although these are rare conditions.

To treat a cramp, stretch the contracted area. This should provide some relief from the pain. Then massage the muscle, applying pressure. Compression, heating pads and a long soak in a warm bath can help as well. Some people find that ice packs are helpful. To prevent muscle cramps, stretch thoroughly before and after working out, drink plenty of fluids and don't over do it.

4) Stress Fractures

Stress fractures, like other overuse injuries, can occur over time. A bone that must withstand repeated stress may sometimes develop a break or a series of small fissures that have the effect of a fracture. In weight training these kinds of fractures occasionally occur, usually in a foot or hand. Using proper technique and limiting the amount of abuse you direct toward any one area of your body can help prevent such an injury. A stress fracture can feel similar to a broken bone, or it can feel like a simple overuse injury.

5) Dislocations

Dislocations usually occur after acute injury, that is, a onetime event that directly causes the injury. A dislocation occurs when the ends of the bones of the joint slip out of their normal place and position. This causes pain, swelling and difficulty using the affected joint. Sometimes a dislocation will injure nearby muscles and ligaments. People with certain diseases, such as rheumatoid arthritis, are more inclined to have this happen. Again, seeking treatment immediately is essential to distinguish a dislocation from a fracture, to determine the extent of damage and to prevent further damage to the surrounding tissues. Usually the dislocation is easily corrected and the area is immobilized for a few days. After this, physical therapy can help bring the affected area back to full use.

Do not resume full speed training until your physician has cleared it. You can reinjure the joint, and even cause permanent damage and disability. Physical therapy may also help strengthen the surrounding muscles and ligaments to prevent a recurrence of a dislocation.

6) Back Injuries

Injuries and strains to the back should always be treated with care because of the possible involvement of the spinal column. Spinal cord injuries are actually quite rare in most sports, and are especially rare in the martial arts, but ruptured disks and the like may occur. Any sharp pain in the back should be heeded. Unexplained tenderness or swelling may be signs of an injury and should be checked out as well.

Avoiding Injury

Although it is not uncommon to have an injury, they can often be prevented if you use your common sense. Any fitness program should include certain stages—the warm-up, stretching, the exercise itself, and the cool down. Including these stages helps prevent lifting injuries from occurring.

Staying Motivated

By picking up this book, you've just taken a big step towards improving your martial arts performance. Adding strength training to your routine can make you a better martial artist faster than you thought possible. But once you embark on a training program designed to build your strength without sacrificing your flexibility, you may find that after a few weeks, it's hard to stay motivated. There are plenty of reasons for this. You may not make a lot of progress at first. You may feel pressed for time. You may feel that other parts of your martial arts training need attention.

Fighting Loss of Motivation

To combat a lack of motivation, try to stay focused on why you started your weight training program. One way to do this is to keep a training log. Not only can you keep track of the exercises you're doing, but you can note your goals and you can see your progress over time. If you don't see progress right away, don't give up. It can take six to eight weeks to begin seeing a difference, but then you'll be surprised at how much strength and endurance you have. Give yourself at least two months before making changes.

Although you may feel other parts of your training program need work too, by following a strength training program, many of those areas will automatically improve. If you're frustrated with your conditioning, a training program will do wonders. If you find it hard to get through a tough class, a training program can build your endurance. If you have trouble with some of your techniques, a training program can give you the strength you need to perform well.

If you feel pressed for time, try a training program that requires you to lift just twice a week. Almost anyone can find a half hour twice a week to get a minimal weight training work out in.

Setting Goals

You are more likely to stick with a weight training program if you have specific goals. If you settle for something vague, like "I want to get in better shape," it will be hard for you to see if you are making any progress toward your goal, and this can be discouraging. Instead, make a list of three to five areas that you want to improve through weight training. It may be that you want stronger abs or stronger arms. You may want to have stronger legs so that you can kick better.

Once you've made your list, decide how you're going to get there. Choose a program or custom tailor one to your needs. Keep your list of goals in mind as you train. You might even write the goals down in your training log.

You can also have specific goals for each exercise. This often helps a martial artist stay focused. For instance, you may want to do ten pull-ups without a spotter. Or fifty push-ups without stopping. Or you may want to bench press your body weight. Or leg press the weight of a used Volvo. Whatever your specific goals for each exercise, write them down where you can see them as you train.

Some people keep two sets of goals, short term goals and long term goals. Their short term goals may be for today or for the next month. They may decide that today they'll do an extra set of each lift. Or they may decide that by the end of the month, they'll lift ten more pounds per lift. Their long term goals may take a few months or a year or even more to achieve. If they can shoulder press eighty pounds today, they may make it a long-term goals to shoulder press one hundred and twenty pounds. Keeping short and long term goals can help you stay motivated in the present while helping you keep in mind what you're striving to achieve.

Avoiding Burnout

Lifters sometimes find that they no longer approach weight training with the same enthusiasm they once had. In fact, they'll do about anything to get out of having to lift or think about lifting.

Often, the reason people feel burnout is because of the stress they put on their bodies when training. Sometimes your body will just tell you to take it easy. The way to avoid physical burnout is to avoid injury and to take care of your body. Make sure you get enough sleep and that you eat well. And don't exercise the same set of muscles every day. Remember to give muscles a chance to heal and repair themselves.

Burnout can occur in beginning lifters who approach training with an enthusiastic, gung-ho attitude. After a couple of weeks, they've exhausted themselves and they don't have a lot to show for their efforts. But sometimes burnout creeps up over time until you wake up one day and you just don't see the point of going to the gym.

Burnout can be avoided—and it can be treated. If you're a beginner, try not to be overenthusiastic about training. Find a schedule you can live with for a long time and then build from there. When you're just starting out, don't hit the weights every day. Do it every other day. You'll stay enthusiastic longer.

If you find that you just can't get enough of lifting, it's okay to go every day. Just keep your workouts reasonable (otherwise you might injure yourself).

If you've been lifting a while, you may hit a plateau where you don't seem to make much progress. For some martial artists, this is not a problem—they're not trying to become body builders. But if it bothers you, consider increasing the challenge of your workouts. (See Chapter Two). Or, choose a different training program. If you've been training using the Endurance Plan, start using the Power Plan. If you've been using the Karate Program, consider changing to the Aikido Program, at least for a little while.

Another approach to take is to read up on weight training, using books and magazines. There are also videos available. These resources may help spark a renewed interest in weight training.

Get Started

The Martial Artist's Training Program is designed to help you become the best martial artists possible. By getting started with the program, you'll be stronger, more flexible, faster and have greater endurance. All of these benefits will make your martial arts experience more rewarding and exciting. The program is flexible enough to accommodate your training goals, whatever they are. All you need to do is pick the plan that's best for you and get started!

Using a Training Log

On the following pages are training log pages. You may write directly in this book (if this is your personal copy) or make as many copies you need for your personal use.

The pages are set up so you can record about a month's worth of workouts on a single page, making it easy to track your progress at a glance. The top row across is for recording the date of the workout session. The left hand column is for recording the name of each exercise. The remaining boxes are for recording the number of reps, and for weight exercises, the number of pounds used.

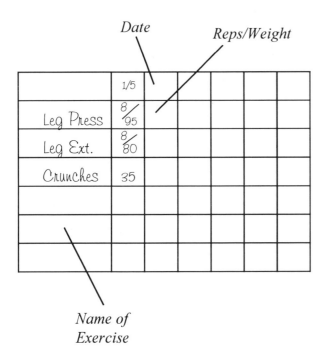

Date *Reps/Weight*

Name of Exercise

Training Log

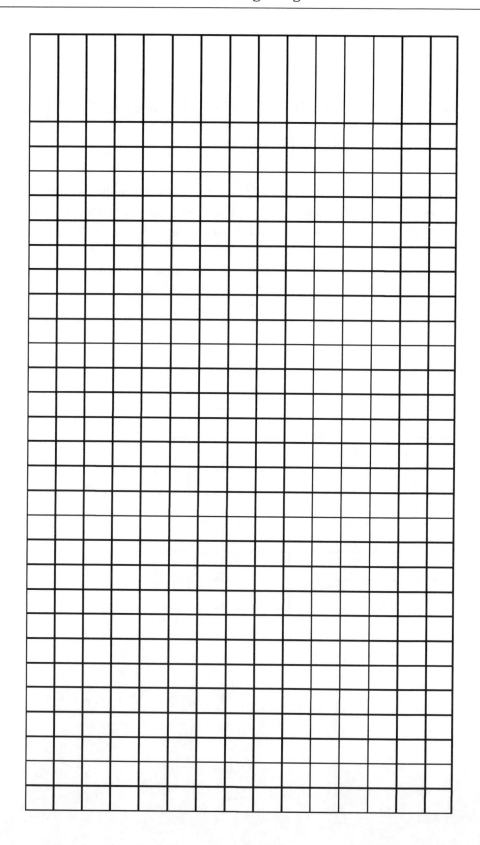

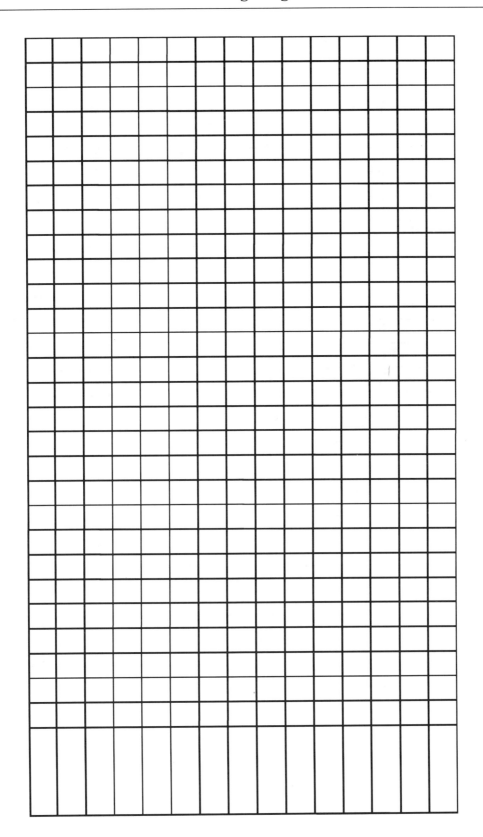

Training Log

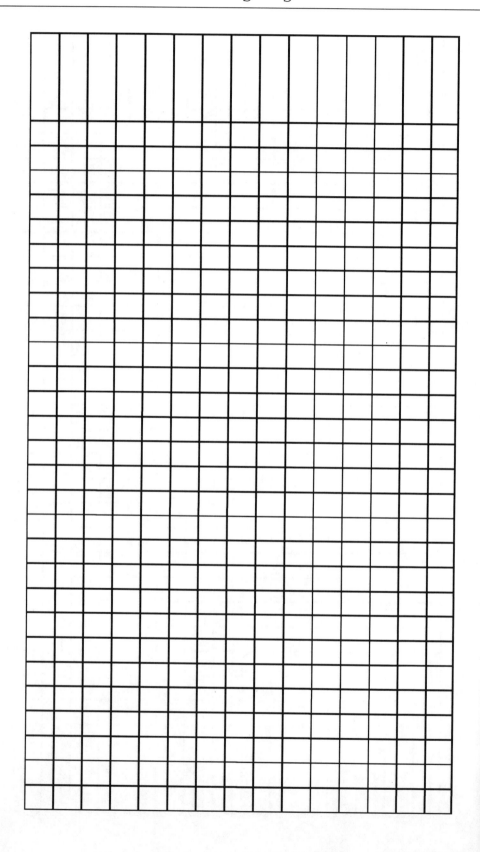

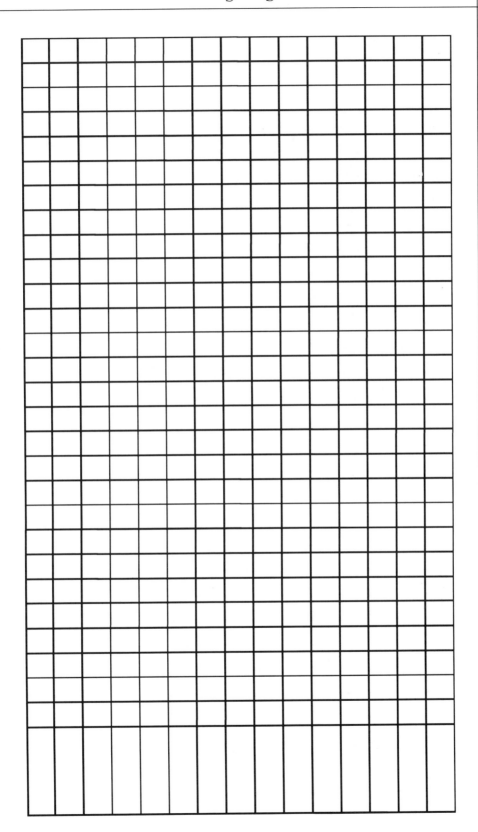

Training Log

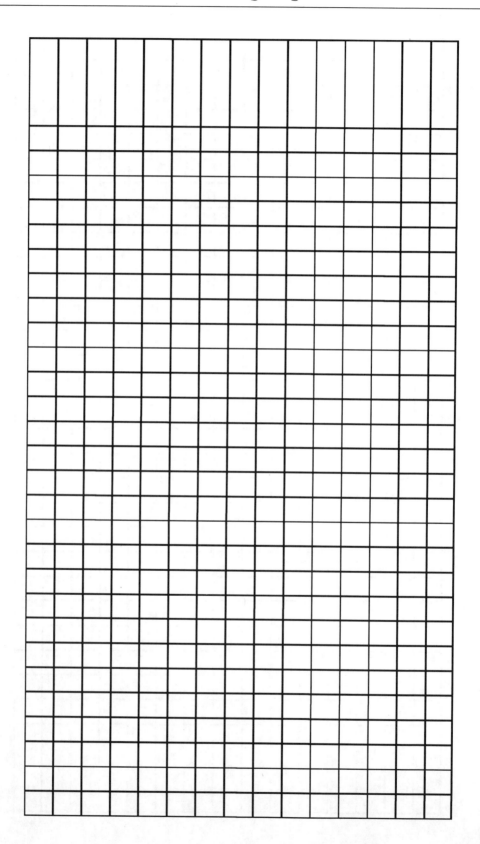

Training Log

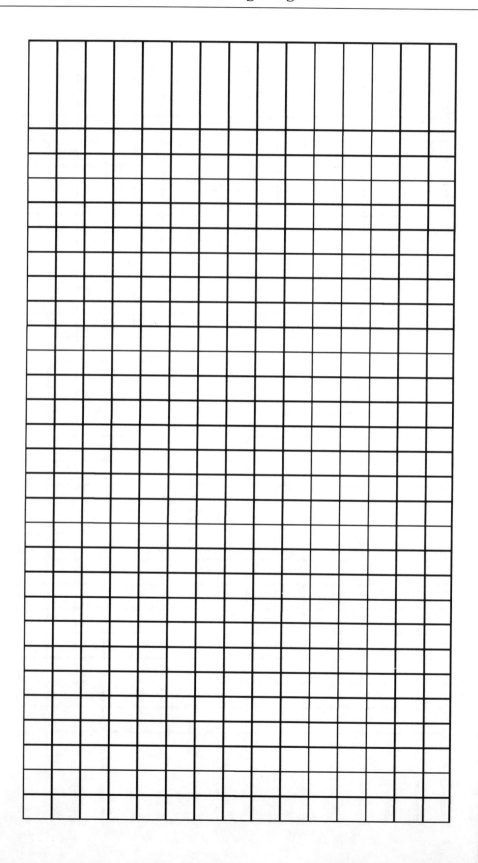

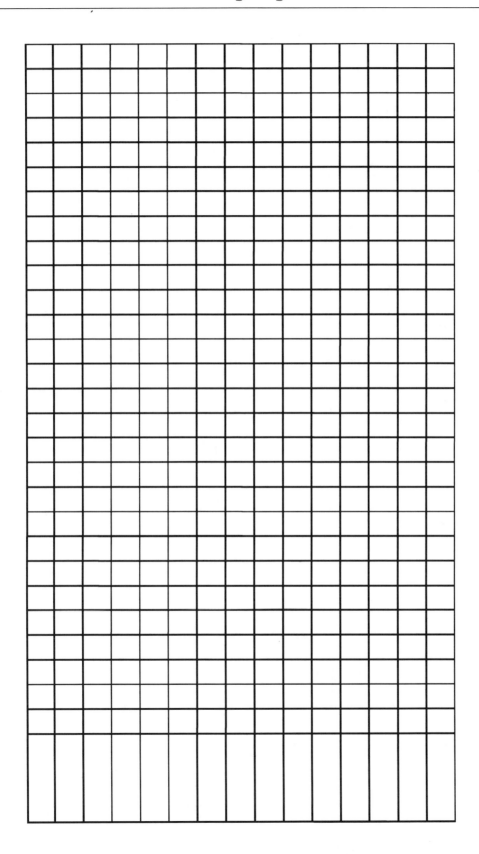

Training Log

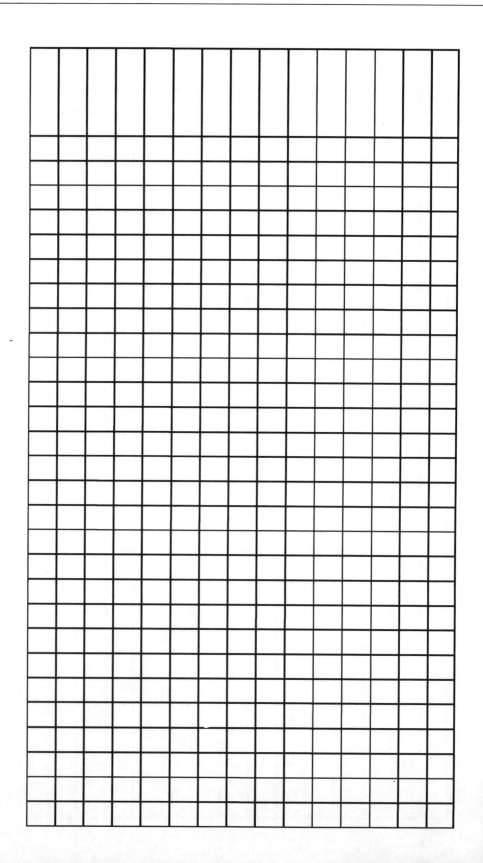

Index

About the Author

Jennifer Lawler is a black belt in Tae Kwon Do. She trains at New Horizons Black Belt Academy of Tae Kwon Do, in Lawrence, Kansas, under Masters Donald and Susan Booth. She also teaches Tae Kwon Do and self-defense classes. She is the author of several books, including "The Martial Arts Encyclopedia" and "Martial Arts for Women: A Practical Guide." She has published numerous articles on martial arts and has a Ph.D in English. She lives in Lawrence with her husband, Bret Kay, who is also a martial artist, and her daughter Jessica (plus two dogs who think they're her children).

Also Available from Turtle Press:

The Martial Arts Training Diary
The Martial Arts Training Diary for Kids
Teaching: The Way of the Master
Combat Strategy
The Art of Harmony
A Guide to Rape Awareness and Prevention
Total MindBody Training
1,001 Ways to Motivate Yourself and Others
Ultimate Fitness through Martial Arts
Taekwondo Kyorugi: Olympic Style Sparring
Launching a Martial Arts School
Advanced Teaching Report
Hosting a Martial Art Tournament
100 Low Cost Marketing Ideas for the Martial Arts School
A Part of the Ribbon: A Time Travel Adventure
Herding the Ox
Neng Da: Super Punches
250 Ways to Make Classes Fun & Exciting
Martial Arts and the Law
Martial Arts for Women
Parents' Guide to Martial Arts

For more information:
Turtle Press
PO Box 290206
Wethersfield CT 06129-206
1-800-77-TURTL
e-mail: sales@turtlepress.com

http://www.turtlepress.com